Inspiring | Educating | Creating | Entertaining

Brimming with creative inspiration, how-to projects, and useful information to enrich your everyday life, quarto.com is a favorite destination for those pursuing their interests and passions.

Rock Point titles are also available at discount for retail, wholesale, promotional, and bulk purchase. For details, contact the Special Sales Manager by email at specialsales@quarto.com or by mail at The Quarto Group, Attn: Special Sales Manager, 100 Cummings Center Suite 265D, Beverly, MA 01915 USA.

10 9 8 7 6

ISBN: 978-1-63106-706-8

Library of Congress Cataloging-in-Publication Data

Names: Uhl, Cassie, author.
Title: The Zenned Out guide to understanding chakras : your handbook to understanding the energy of your chakra system / by Cassie Uhl.
Description: New York, NY : Rock Point Publishing, 2020. | Series: Zenned out | Summary: "The Zenned Out Guide to Understanding Chakras is your essential introduction to restoring healing and balance. Part of the Zenned Out series, this book includes easy-to-digest actionable steps to enable readers to get started right away"-- Provided by publisher.
Identifiers: LCCN 2020012102 (print) | LCCN 2020012103 (ebook) | ISBN 9781631067068 (hardcover) | ISBN 9780760367841 (ebook)
Subjects: LCSH: Chakras. | Healing--Popular works.
Classification: LCC BF1442.C53 U35 2020 (print) | LCC BF1442.C53 (ebook) | DDC 131--dc23
LC record available at https://lccn.loc.gov/2020012102
LC ebook record available at https://lccn.loc.gov/2020012103

PUBLISHER: Rage Kindelsperger
CREATIVE DIRECTOR: Laura Drew
MANAGING EDITOR: Cara Donaldson
EDITOR: Keyla Pizarro-Hernández
COVER AND INTERIOR DESIGN: Sydney Martenis

Printed in China

THE ZENNED OUT GUIDE TO

UNDERSTANDING CHAKRAS

YOUR HANDBOOK TO UNDERSTANDING THE ENERGY OF THE CHAKRA SYSTEM

CASSIE UHL

ROCK
POINT

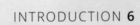

◦◁ INTRODUCTION ▷◦

Your chakras connect to every aspect of your life. They provide access to the infinite energy of the cosmos, the divine spark within you, and the regenerative qualities of the earth. Chakras are spinning wheels within you that are constantly moving and transforming your energy. When I say "energy," I'm referring to subtle energy. Subtle energy is the unseen force you sense when your intuition is piqued. It is the energy of emotion, thought, and inner knowing.

You have an entire body system designated to these unseen energies, and your chakras are at the heart of it. Your subtle body is the unseen system that's responsible for the flow of energy within and around you. It holds the pieces of you that are eternal, the parts that will live on when your physical body dies.

Perhaps the idea of an energy body is new to you, or maybe you've always had an inclination that something was there. There are so many forces that work within us and around us that we can't see. Gravity, sound, and magnetism are all invisible but very real energies. Just because you can't see the chakras doesn't mean you can discount their existence.

YOUR CHAKRAS CONTROL THE FLOW OF ENERGY BETWEEN YOUR PHYSICAL BODY AND YOUR SPIRIT BODY.

The chakras, and similar energy centers, have been recognized by humans since the beginning of written history. Many healers claim to be able to see the swirling energy of the chakra system, and anyone can learn how to feel the energy of the chakras. Science is now showing us that even solid objects are made up of energy.

Every person and thing you come into contact with releases energy. The chakra system is constantly filtering through the energy that you encounter, either storing it or releasing it. When the stream of energy within your chakra system is flowing freely, it can move through your body with ease, and all aspects of your mental, physical, and spiritual body will be in alignment. The chakras can work independently, but they are the most powerful when they are aligned and working together.

In this book, I will share a foundation to better understand your subtle body (energy body) and a modern approach to working with the seven main chakras. You will learn how to assess the health and energy of your seven primary chakras and discover tools to engage with them in meaningful ways.

BENEFITS OF WORKING WITH THE CHAKRA SYSTEM

♦ You will become the conscious observer of your life and have a better understanding of your purpose on earth.

♦ You will increase your intuitive abilities and find deep peace.

♦ You will learn how to speak openly and honestly to propel the human species into higher states of being.

♦ You will experience a greater sense of love for yourself and others.

♦ You will access an internal fire of energy and strength to transform your life for the better.

♦ You will learn how to flow through the ups and downs of life with ease and access more pleasure.

♦ You will decrease your anxiety and fears through a powerful sense of safety.

The information I share with you is based on my in-depth research of chakras, and most importantly, my personal experiences working with them. However, the best way for you to understand and use these unseen energies is to experience them for yourself. This is why I've offered recipes or meditations in each chapter to encourage you to experience the energy of each chakra fully. When you understand the unique energy of the seven primary chakras, you will be able to apply their energy to specific life situations.

When you access the energy of your chakras, you, too, will be able to improve your life in every aspect. The benefits you receive from this journey won't stop with you, either: they will spill over into family, friends, and even strangers you encounter. Your healing will cause a ripple effect that will help others heal, too.

The chakras have a rich history, and there's a reference to different energy systems, like the chakras, in nearly every human culture. There are many viewpoints about our modern understanding of chakras. Let's take a quick look at the history of the chakra system to gain a better understanding of modern interpretations.

HISTORY OF CHAKRAS

In Sanskrit, the word *chakra* translates to "wheel," which is first seen in written history within the Vedas, ancient Indian texts that are the basis of Hinduism. The Vedic texts are some of the oldest written scriptures, spanning from 1500 to 500 BCE. Many believe the information shared in the Vedic texts is actually far older because it was passed down orally for centuries prior to being written down.

Even in our modern world, there are few individuals who fully understand Sanskrit. It's not a surprise that there have been many interpretations of the chakra system. Beyond this early written record of the chakras, there are a variety of cultures that reference chakras or similar energy points within the body. Mention of chakras can be found in a variety of Buddhist texts, mysticism from the Far East, and several indigenous cultures.

If you begin to dive deeper into the history of chakras, you will find that the numbers of them vary tremendously. Some texts suggest as many as 114 total chakras, and some suggest as few as two. I point all of this out to impress upon you that the seven-chakra system, as we understand it today, is modern and not definitive.

If you've had a previous introduction to the chakra system, you've probably seen them portrayed in colorful rainbow order. The colors associated with each chakra, as often seen today, is an entirely modern interpretation that came about in the 1970s.

Some early drawings of different chakra systems show colors that align with the modern chakra system. Still, many either don't align or don't offer a specific color at all. This is one example of how the chakras have evolved over time.

Knowledge of chakras and subtle energy has traveled over centuries, across continents, and through various languages. Of course, our understanding of the chakra system has changed, and will continue to change, just as we evolve as a species. In this book, I focus on the seven-chakra system from both a Hindu and a modern perspective. Because I am a yoga practitioner and teacher, my education is rooted in Hinduism. And because I was born and live in the United States, my knowledge of the chakra system has been filtered through a modern Western lens.

Nevertheless, there are certain facets of the chakras from the ancient Vedic texts that have persevered throughout time, some of which I share here. If you are interested in the origins and history of the chakra system, I encourage you to research the topic further, and I provide a reference list at the end of the book. There is much to be learned from the ancient wisdom of our energy systems.

MY INTRODUCTION
TO CHAKRA ENERGY

When I began meditating at a young age, I felt several physical sensations in my body. Sitting in my room, falling deeper into meditation, I would feel a sensation to straighten and align my spine. Sometimes, it felt like there were unseen energies at the base of my spine and the top of my head stretching me out. This sensation would always cause me to drop deeper into meditation. I would then experience a warm, tingling sensation all over my body, or begin to feel like my physical body wasn't even there!

I had no proper training in meditation, chakras, or the subtle body when I began my meditation journey. All I knew was that it felt good and connected me to a source greater than myself. As my spiritual journey progressed, I eventually came across the chakra system. My meditation experiences immediately made sense, and I understood that through my meditation practice, I was aligning and balancing my chakras.

After I made this connection, I began working more consciously with my chakras. I work with my chakras and energy body every morning during my meditation practice, and I often focus on them throughout the day. Through my business, Zenned Out, I've been handcrafting jewelry specifically for each chakra and sharing tips and tools for accessing their energy on our blog since 2012. I hope that my love for the subtle body and the chakras lights a spark within you to experiment with your energy and deepen your spiritual practice.

◦◁ HOW TO USE THIS BOOK ▷◦

I've devoted an entire chapter in this book to understanding the subtle body system. If there's a chapter that you dedicate yourself to reading fully, let it be chapter 1. When you have a deep understanding of the subtle body system, working with the chakras will be more meaningful. After you read the first chapter, you can read the entire book from cover to cover, but you may feel called to jump around from chakra to chakra. Either option is fine.

As I mentioned earlier, I've included both traditional Hindu and modern Western information on each chakra. Honor what feels good and right to you. If you feel called to dive deeper into the teachings of Hinduism and explore the goddesses and gods associated with each chakra, I encourage you to do the research. If you feel content with the modern meanings, that is okay, too.

◂◞ CORRESPONDENCES ◟▸

Correspondences are symbols and objects that share similar energy, and you'll see correspondences listed for each chakra chapter. I work with correspondences in my practice every day and find understanding them to be a valuable tool for energy and ritual work. The correspondences I offer are meant to help you deepen your understanding of each chakra and call upon their energies in your spiritual practice.

·◦◗ TIP ◖◦·

You do not need to fully understand the correspondences to work with and enjoy each chakra. Think of the correspondences as optional bonus information!

Here's a little bit more information about each of the correspondences.

♦ **Petals**: The number of petals of each chakra has a couple of meanings. First, the number of petals increases (aside from the third eye chakra) for each chakra as they ascend up the spine. There's an increase in frequency with each chakra, therefore the number of petals increases as well. Secondly, traditional Hindu chakras include a Sanskrit (ancient Indian language) letter in each petal of each chakra. The study of the Sanskrit language is rich and deep. I suggest digging deeper into the study of the Sanskrit if you feel called to it.

♦ **Bija Mantra**: The sound associated with the chakra. I share more about using the Bija Mantras on page 17.

♦ **Colors**: The traditional and modern colors associated with each chakra vary greatly. As I mentioned in the introduction, the modern colors associated with the seven chakras came about in the 1970's. Trust your intuition when deciding whether to work with the traditional or modern colors for each chakra, they're both valid.

♦ **Element**: The five elements are earth, water, fire, air, and ether (spirit). Each element carries a unique energy and, similar to the chakras, each element is less and less dense from earth to spirit. For the four lower chakras (root, sacral, solar plexus, and heart) the traditional and modern elements align. For the three upper chakras, the elements begin to diverge for the traditional and modern correspondences. In the traditional Hindu Chakras, the elements assigned to each chakra stop at the throat chakra with ether. In order to assign an element to each chakra I've chosen to label the upper three chakras with elements. Similar to the chakra colors, you can decide to honor the element for each chakra, traditional or modern, that rings true for you.

Crystals, zodiac, planets, numbers, plants, and runes: These correspondences are commonly used by a variety of spiritual practices (astrology, Wicca, witchcraft, numerology, etc.) and may be helpful for connecting with chakra energy in different ways.

Every chakra has a meaning and purpose, I like to refer to this as its essence. Understanding the essence of each chakra will make it easier for you to know which one you need to work with for different issues you may be experiencing. For example, if you're feeling disconnected from your physical body, you will want to focus on the root chakra because its essence deals with physicality.

In addition to the essence of each chakra, there are mantras or short phrases that are associated with every chakra as well. The mantras related to each one can be used as a tool to feel connected with the chakra. You could do this by repeating a mantra during meditation or by writing a mantra on a card that you will see daily. These suggestions can be applied to the essence and mantras associated with each chakra.

Beyond the essence and mantras associated with the chakras there are a host of other ways to connect with and balance each of them. I offer illustrated guides for each chakra as a quick way for you to reference tools for connecting with and healing your chakras. You'll be able to read more in-depth ways to work with them later on in each chapter.

For each chakra I share a suggested chant, crystals, scents, and color visualization. Here are suggestions for working with these different tools.

♦ **Chanting**: Each chakra is associated with a sound, which can be accessed by chanting the Bija Mantra (also called "seed sound"). To connect with the chakras through sound, you can chant the Bija Mantra of the chakra of your choice aloud during meditation or softly to yourself throughout your day.

♦ **Crystals**: Connect with the crystals associated with each chakra by wearing them, holding them during meditation, carrying them in your pocket or bra, or sleeping with them under your pillow or on your nightstand.

♦ **Scents**: Work with scent for each chakra by diffusing essential oils, wearing essential oils diluted with a carrier oil (jojoba or fractionated coconut oil work well), or by burning incense or loose herbs.

♦ **Color visualization**: As you'll see in this book, there are colors associated with all of the seven chakras. You can visualize the color associated with each one to connect with the energy of the chakra. Color visualizations can be done during meditation by visualizing the color around your body. Alternatively, they can be done anytime throughout your day by closing your eyes and visualizing the color of the chakra you're trying to connect with.

CHAPTER 1
THE SUBTLE BODY

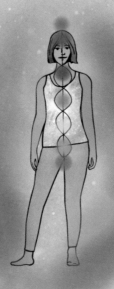

Your chakras are part of a more extensive system called your subtle body system. Your subtle body is, generally, not visible to the naked eye. There are some people born with the gift of clairvoyance, which means they can see subtle energy; others can learn how to do this. But for the vast majority of us, the subtle body is something that is felt but not seen.

The subtle body connects directly to the physical body. One cannot live without the other. The subtle and physical bodies are intrinsically linked and affect each other moment to moment. When dis-ease presents in the subtle body—for example, prolonged stress or lack of love—it will eventually manifest in the physical body. Or, if the physical body experiences trauma, the trauma can be stored in the subtle body. Dis-ease is a term often used in the wellness and spiritual community as an alternative to "disease," to mean lack of harmony or wholeness within the body and subtle body.

When you understand your subtle body and your chakras, you will gain a deeper understanding of your entire being. Parts of the subtle body will stay with you even after death; they are part of the soul and are timeless. These are some reasons why it is so important to be aware of and able to connect with the energy of your chakras.

There are three primary parts of the subtle body. The nadis (channels of energy), the chakras (wheels of energy), and the aura (energy that radiates outside of the body). All three systems are intimately connected to each other and the physical body.

NADIS

Nadis are channels that carry energy, or *prana*, throughout the subtle body. Think of your nadis as a circulatory system for energy. The word *nadi* in Sanskrit translates to "movement." To give you an idea of how prevalent the nadi system is within your subtle body, there are said to be a total of 72,000 nadis within the human body.

Just as there are primary blood vessels within your physical body, there are also primary nadis within your subtle body. The three primary nadis are the ida, pingala, and sushumna, and they interact with the chakra system the most.

The ida and the pingala nadi begin in the root chakra and weave their way up the sushumna nadi until they meet in the third eye chakra. The seven primary chakras are lined up on the sushumna nadi.

To better understand ida and pingala, let's take a closer look at the energy they're associated with. The best way to understand them is to look at them through the lenses of lunar and solar energy. See the graphics on pages 21 to 22 for a breakdown of each.

This central channel, the sushumna nadi, is the key to enlightenment and liberation. It is through the sushumna nadi that the energy of the chakras connects and aligns, enabling you to become one with the cosmos. Though enlightenment may be the end goal, it can take many lifetimes to attain it.

THE THREE PRIMARY NADIS

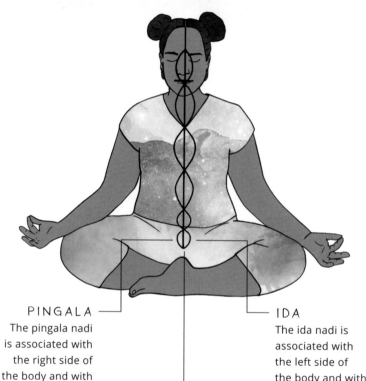

PINGALA
The pingala nadi
is associated with
the right side of
the body and with
masculine energy.

IDA
The ida nadi is
associated with
the left side of
the body and with
feminine energy.

SUSHUMNA
The sushumna nadi begins at
the base of the spine and runs
up the center of the spine
through the top of the head.
This nadi is associated with
enlightenment and is where
the chakras live.

·◦◁ SUN AND MOON ENERGIES ▷◦·

IDA AND THE MOON
Yin, feminine, passive, water, reflective, receiving, healing

PINGALA AND THE SUN
Yang, masculine, active, fire, giving, energy

THE CHAKRAS

The chakras are at the center of the subtle body system. They are in constant motion, exchanging energy between the nadis and the aura. It's easy to see how important the chakra system is in the context of the subtle body system. When the chakras are out of balance, the entire subtle body is affected, which will eventually manifest in the physical body. These wheels of energy are all over your body. Just like the nadis, there are far more chakras than the seven primary chakras. As mentioned earlier, some early texts suggest there are 114 chakras within the subtle body, but in this book, I'll be focusing on the seven primary chakras.

Even though chakras are often displayed as flat wheels on top of the body, this is far from the truth. The chakras are three-dimensional vortexes that radiate outside the front and the back of the body. The vortex shape of the chakras enables them to process through the energy you come into contact with and expel energy you don't need. We'll dive deeper into the spins of the chakras and how to determine their health later on.

The reach of chakra energy goes beyond the subtle body. Each of the seven primary chakras relates to physical parts of the body, including prominent nerve bundles, glands, and organs. Gifted healers and clairvoyants have witnessed these connections and use the information they see in the chakras and the auras to heal and diagnose physical ailments. For instance, Dr. Valerie Hunt, who was well known for influencing dance and movement therapy, performed experiments to confirm the existence of the chakras using electromyography. Her experiments showed that there are increased energies within the physical body in areas that correlate to the seven chakras.

On a nonphysical level, each chakra also corresponds to light and sound. Light and sound are both vibratory frequencies. This is easier to see with sound because we can actually see the vibratory effects of sound. Light, on the other hand, vibrates at an extremely high rate. As we move up the chakra system from the base to the crown, the vibration increases. The sounds and colors associated with each chakra increase in vibration as well.

THE SEVEN CHAKRAS

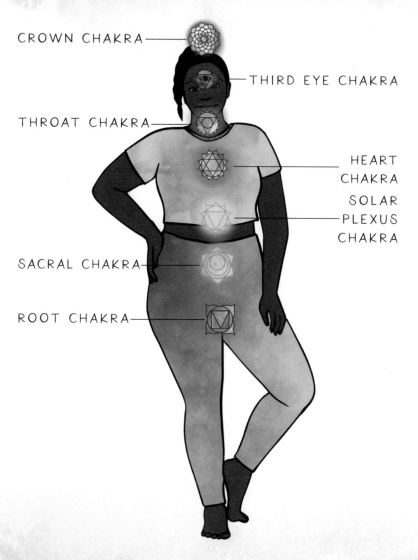

CROWN CHAKRA

THIRD EYE CHAKRA

THROAT CHAKRA

HEART CHAKRA

SOLAR PLEXUS CHAKRA

SACRAL CHAKRA

ROOT CHAKRA

⊶ THE HUMAN AURA ⊷

Auras are colorful electromagnetic fields of energy around the body and the outermost part of your subtle body system. The aura can extend several feet out from your body and is continually shifting and changing in color. This energetic field of energy is the expression of your subtle body, which is generated through your chakras. Each part of your subtle body is linked to the other, creating a vast and beautiful network of energy.

The aura is comprised of seven layers, and this is no coincidence. Each layer of your aura corresponds with one of the seven chakras. The etheric layer of the aura is the one closest to your body. It connects with the root chakra. The casual layer of the aura is farthest from the body and connects with the crown chakra. The color of the aura is directly affected by the health and well-being of each chakra. If you are experiencing a great deal of anger, this will show up in your aura as red.

It's more common to see auras than chakras. Some people are born with the ability, and it is possible to learn. Few experienced healers and psychics can see the energy of auras and even the seven chakras with their own eyes. Being able to see the chakras is far less common and more difficult than seeing auras. If you're interested in learning how to see the energy of the subtle body, I suggest beginning with the aura. The first layer of the aura, the etheric layer, is the easiest to see because it is the densest. It often appears as a white, blue, or gray ring of light around the body.

CHAPTER 2
THE ROOT CHAKRA

MULADHARA

SUPPORT

The root chakra offers primal energy, one that keeps you alive. It is here, at the base of the spine, that the foundation for all the other chakras is built. Your root chakra is your direct link to the earth and your ability to be grounded and feel secure. A healthy connection to the earth will offer you a deep sense of safety and protection that is necessary for your well-being and survival. If your root chakra is neglected, all the other chakras will suffer as a result.

The location of your root chakra is the base of your spine or perineum. It is the starting point of the ida, pingala, and sushumna nadis, which we discussed earlier. The fact that this chakra is the starting point of these powerful energy channels indicates the incredible importance of the root chakra.

On a physical level, your root chakra connects to the adrenal glands. The adrenal glands control our "fight-or-flight" response, which is our most basic survival instinct. Without our adrenals, we would not be here. As a species, this is something we're still navigating. The need to protect ourselves from wild animals and hunt for food, at least for most of us, is no longer an issue. However, our adrenal glands have not quite caught up. Stressing about a deadline or lack of time can trigger the same fight-or-flight response, even though they're not life-or-death situations. We still need a strong foundation and connection to the earth to feel safe, even in our modern world.

ESSENCE

SAFETY, STABILITY, GROUNDEDNESS,
MATERIALITY, PHYSICALITY

MANTRAS

THE EARTH SUPPORTS ME.

I HAVE EVERYTHING I NEED.

I AM SAFE AND HELD WITHIN
MOTHER EARTH.

I AM CENTERED, AND I AM STRONG.

I SET BOUNDARIES TO
PROTECT MYSELF.

CONNECTING WITH
THE ROOT CHAKRA

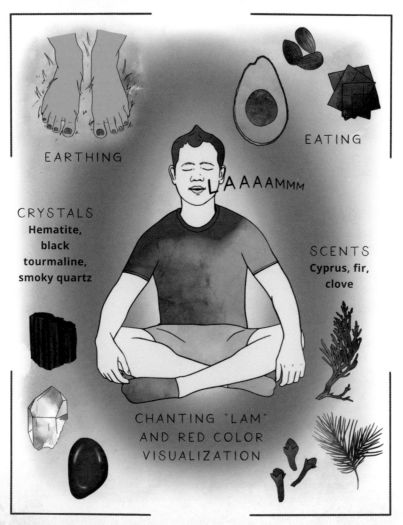

EARTHING

EATING

CRYSTALS
Hematite, black tourmaline, smoky quartz

LAAAAMMM

SCENTS
Cyprus, fir, clove

CHANTING "LAM"
AND RED COLOR
VISUALIZATION

THE PURPOSE OF
THE ROOT CHAKRA

Deep within your root chakra is where your most basic survival instincts reside. Your root chakra sustains you during emergencies and times of intense stress. It is through the wisdom of your root chakra that we persevere as a species. Without our connection to our root chakra, we lose our ability to care for ourselves on the most basic level—individually and as a species.

Another primary function of your root chakra is to filter out stagnant and toxic energy from your chakra system and aura. When you're connected to the earth through your root chakra, you're able to cycle through your energy more efficiently and release negative energy into the earth. Think of your root chakra as an energy filtration system, always bringing up supportive energy from the earth, then releasing negative energy you don't need back into the earth. Don't worry: the earth can easily absorb and transmute all of the negative energy you send its way!

Lastly, your root chakra is the seat of Shakti, or kundalini energy. According to yogic teachings, kundalini energy lies dormant in the root chakra; if awakened, it will aid in total liberation and enlightenment. Kundalini energy rises from your root chakra, working its way up through all the other chakras and ultimately joining with the opposing energy (Shiva) from the heavens. Awakening this kundalini energy requires a healthy root chakra.

THE ROOT CHAKRA
AS A FOUNDATION

Many people hold the belief that that which is higher is better. We see this often in the spiritual community. There's an association with the higher chakras being better or more positive. This might be the case if you were already in spirit form, but you're not— none of us is right now. While on the earth, in human form, you are a physical being. Physicality is the language of this world. We have to embrace and understand our physicality in order to progress.

SPIRITUAL GROWTH REQUIRES YOU TO HAVE A STRONG FOUNDATION.

All of the lower chakras, especially the root chakra, are essential for growth. Without a strong foundation, you will not be able to access the higher states of consciousness. As you'll see in the chapters about the higher chakras, it is necessary to have a strong foundation in all of the lower chakras to enhance your intuition and experience enlightenment.

ROOT CHAKRA CORRESPONDENCES

◁〜 TRADITIONAL HINDU CORRESPONDENCES 〜▷

- ♦ **Petals**: 4

- ♦ **Bija Mantra**: Lam

- ♦ **Colors**: Gold, red

- ♦ **Element**: Earth

◁〜 MODERN WESTERN CORRESPONDENCES 〜▷

- ♦ **Moon Phase**: Dark moon

- ♦ **Element**: Earth

- ♦ **Color**: Red

- ♦ **Crystals**: Hematite, black tourmaline, smoky quartz

- ♦ **Zodiac**: Capricorn, Taurus, Virgo

- ♦ **Planets**: Earth, Saturn

- ♦ **Number**: 8

- ♦ **Plants**: Cypress, fir, clove

- ♦ **Runes**: Nauthiz, Uruz

⊲ BALANCED ROOT CHAKRA ⊳

When your root chakra is balanced, you move through life with a calm confidence that your needs will always be met. Feeling fully supported arises from a firm reliance on the earth and your ability to care for yourself. Those with a balanced root chakra do not shy away from their physicality or experiencing the physical world.

Signs of a balanced root chakra:

♦ I feel safe and protected.

♦ I feel supported and believe that what's meant for me will come to me.

♦ I enjoy being outside.

♦ I feel connected to my body.

♦ I set boundaries with ease to honor and protect myself.

♦ I enjoy the physical world.

OVERACTIVE ROOT CHAKRA

When we become obsessed with the physical world, it means that our root chakra is overactive. An overactive root chakra is easy to identify because it feels like the physical world. You can probably think of some people you know who may have an overactive root chakra. Feelings of lack and greed are common associations with an overactive root chakra.

Signs of an overactive root chakra:

- ♦ I am usually angry.

- ♦ I hoard money and objects.

- ♦ I am scared that I won't have enough of what I need.

- ♦ I tend to overeat.

TIPS FOR BALANCING
AN OVERACTIVE
ROOT CHAKRA

- ◆ Work with heart-healing stones like rose quartz, malachite, and green moss agate.

- ◆ If angry, move your body to release the anger, in a way that resonates with you. You could dance, go for a walk, do some yoga, run, or even give yourself a massage.

- ◆ Meditate on the heart chakra and visualize a cooling green color around your body. There is a heart chakra breathing technique on pages 92 to 93 that can serve as a helpful guide for doing a heart chakra meditation. As you practice the breathing technique you can visualize a light green color around your body to help cool an overactive root chakra.

UNDERACTIVE ROOT CHAKRA

Have you ever felt drawn to spend more time in nature? Most of us have experienced this sensation, especially when it's not possible to be outside during times of intense heat and cold. But this can also happen if we neglect our need to connect with the earth. When you experience this calling from Mother Earth to connect with her, it is a sign that your root chakra is disconnected.

Signs of an underactive root chakra:

♦ I feel flighty, spacey, or anxious.

♦ I have trouble sleeping because my mind is racing.

♦ I feel disconnected from my body.

♦ I have trouble finishing tasks because I can't focus.

BALANCING AND OPENING
YOUR ROOT CHAKRA

The earth has a powerful electromagnetic field that connects with your root chakra. When healthy and open, your root chakra can pull energy up from the earth, through your feet, and into your body. The energy from the earth is critical for the well-being of your entire body, physically, mentally, and spiritually. We live in a busy world that's often disconnected from nature. It is your root chakra that suffers the most from this disconnection, which can result in feelings of anxiety, fear, and lack.

Fortunately, there are so many ways to connect with Mother Earth, even if you live in a climate that makes it difficult. Making physical contact with the earth is one of the best ways to ground yourself. Next time you're outside, stand on the ground with your bare feet. Scientific studies have been conducted about the health benefits of making contact with the earth in this way, or "earthing." The earth emits negative ions, which have a very positive effect on our bodies.

Your mind is also a powerful tool to visualize a connection to the earth. You can perform a grounding root chakra meditation (see pages 42 to 43), which you can use anytime you're feeling anxious or scared.

There are many ways to open and balance the root chakra. A quick way to help ground yourself is to eat some protein or chocolate. Beyond these tools, there are several crystals and herbs that can help you heal your root chakra.

HERBS FOR BALANCING YOUR ROOT CHAKRA

Earthy scents like pine, cypress, and patchouli will all benefit the root chakra. Burn or diffuse any of these scents for a reminder of your connection to the earth. Scent is another potent tool for the root chakra because scents in their natural form come from Mother Earth. Though some scents may smell "earthier," all scents from Mother Earth will offer you some grounding. Clove is associated with protection, so it will also serve you well, especially when you feel your root chakra is compromised.

CRYSTALS TO BALANCE YOUR ROOT CHAKRA

Crystals help balance the root chakra because they come from the earth. Grounding crystals are great to wear or carry if you know you're going to do something that may trigger your sense of safety. You can also hold grounding crystals in your hands during any meditation to help you stay connected to the earth. Because the root chakra deals with the physical world, a physical tool like a crystal from the earth serves as a strong reminder to be aware of your connection to the earth and your root chakra. Any dark-colored crystal will offer grounding energy.

CRYSTALS FOR
THE ROOT CHAKRA

HEMATITE FOR GROUNDING
Hematite is an incredible grounding stone. Physically, it is quite a heavy stone, which enhances its sense of grounding. Hematite shields the aura and helps align the subtle body with the physical body.

BLACK TOURMALINE FOR PROTECTION
Black tourmaline is both protective and cleansing. This is an ideal stone to use if you live or work with people whom you find triggering. It will help keep you grounded and remove any negative energy from your surroundings.

SMOKY QUARTZ FOR BALANCE
Smoky quartz is grounding and balancing. Because it is in the quartz family, it has a higher vibration, but it still connects deeply to earth energy. This is an ideal stone to work with if you already have a balanced root chakra.

GARNET FOR ENERGY
When you need help getting into your body and experiencing your physicality, garnet is your stone. It is grounding and energizing. This is a great stone for people with an underactive root chakra.

GROUNDING MEDITATION

1. Find a comfortable sitting position.

2. If you have any grounding crystals handy, like hematite, black tourmaline, jasper, garnet, or smoky quartz, you can hold them or place them near you.

3. Close your eyes and take a few moments to notice your breath.

4. Thoughts may come into your mind, and that's okay. Just notice the thought, and then return to your breath.

5. Inhale, sending your breath lower into your belly, then exhale. Increase the length of your inhales and exhales each time you breathe in and out.

6. Begin to visualize that you're sitting in your favorite nature spot. If you don't have one, make it up and make it lush.

7. As you sit in your imaginary lush landscape, imagine your root chakra swirling and glowing red.

8. From your root chakra, visualize a beam of red energy anchoring deep into the earth.

9. Ask the earth to hold you and give you strength.

10. Stay in this safe, grounded space for as long as you'd like.

11. When you're ready to leave the meditation, thank the earth for her energy and strength, and open your eyes.

PROTECTION CHARM BAG

The heart of the root chakra is feeling safe. When you feel safe, you feel free to explore your desires and express yourself. One way to add a sense of safety to your environment is by creating a protection charm bag. Charm bags are magickal tools that hold a variety of items, all aligned with the same purpose. The best thing about them is how portable they are!

You'll need:

- ♦ A little piece of hematite, black tourmaline, or smoky quartz

- ♦ A few pieces of dried clove

- ♦ Salt of any kind

- ♦ A symbol of protection. Any symbol that represents protection to you will work. Some suggestions are the evil eye, hamsa hand, cross, pentacle, or the algiz rune. Your symbol can be added in the bag or placed on the outside as a reminder of its purpose.

- ♦ A small black bag or pouch

To make:

1. Place all of your items in your bag.

2. Close your eyes and ask that the bag protect you and keep you safe.

3. Hang your protection charm bag in your home, carry it with you, or place it on your desk.

CHAPTER 3

THE SACRAL CHAKRA

SVADHISTHANA

SWEETNESS

The sacral chakra is an intense area of movement, creativity, and pleasure. You can experience deep pleasure by accessing the energy of the sacral chakra, but also intense emotion. The sacral chakra is located below the belly button and above the pubic bone. For women, the sacral chakra resides at the womb. If you are a woman but do not have a womb, or are a man, the sacral chakra is in the location that the womb would be.

Translations of Svadhisthana vary from "one's own abode" to "to taste sweet." Though both translations are valid, because this chakra deals with experiencing pleasure, I feel that "sweetness" offers a more accurate description of this chakra. If you feel more called to the translation of "one's own abode," it is also accurate.

The sacral chakra encourages us to experience and revel in our five senses. It is also the place where we experience and move through our emotions. There is a fine line of balance within the sacral chakra. As physical beings, we desire pleasurable experiences but can become easily consumed by them. The chakra above the sacral chakra is the solar plexus chakra. The solar plexus chakra deals with willpower (among other things). Because the sacral chakra teaches us to enjoy pleasure, we next need to learn willpower so we're not constantly consumed by our desires. It's no surprise that the solar plexus chakra follows this chakra!

The element associated with this chakra is water, which can be both soothing and destructive. Water represents a constant flow of energy that's always available to you. If you imagine a stream of water with rocks in it, the water flows around the stones with ease.

ESSENCE

MOVEMENT, PLEASURE, SENSUALITY,
EMOTIONS, FLOW

MANTRAS

I HONOR MY FEELINGS.

I ALLOW MYSELF TO FEEL PLEASURE.

I AM IN FLOW WITH LIFE.

I AM A SEXUAL BEING.

I EXPRESS MYSELF WITH MY BODY.

CONNECTING WITH THE SACRAL CHAKRA

WATER

MOVEMENT

CRYSTALS
Carnelian, opal, moonstone

CHANTING "VAM" AND ORANGE COLOR VISUALIZATION

SCENTS
Ylang-ylang, sandalwood, cinnamon

PLEASURE

THE PURPOSE OF THE
SACRAL CHAKRA

The sacral chakra has several vital roles. It is responsible for your ability to experience pleasure and work through your emotions. On a more superficial level, the sacral chakra aids in your ability to be creative, be in relationships, and be in flow with life.

Through opening and balancing the sacral chakra, you will learn how to be in a healthy romantic relationship. Touch, pleasure, and sexuality are critical parts of experiencing the energy of the sacral chakra. When we deny ourselves intimacy, it will display as an imbalance within the sacral chakra. You might also see an increase in rage or withdrawal from social activities.

BE IN FLOW WITH EVERY EMOTION AND RIDE EACH ONE LIKE A WAVE, SEEING IT THROUGH TO THE END.

Beyond sensuality, we must be able to express our emotions in healthy ways. The sacral chakra gives us the tools to do this. When we repress our desires and emotions, they often come out negatively. Through this chakra, we learn how to express ourselves. Emotional expression is so much more than having a good cry. The sacral chakra teaches us how to fully experience emotions so they can leave the subtle and physical body.

As you'll read later in this book, the throat chakra also deals with self-expression. The self-expression of the sacral chakra is more primal than that of the throat chakra. Rather than expressing yourself through words, if you have an open and flowing sacral chakra, you'll be able to express yourself through movement, visual arts, or dance.

THE SACRAL CHAKRA AND FEMININITY

The sacral chakra carries a strong connection to feminine energy. Both men and women have this chakra, and even though it corresponds to femininity, both masculine and feminine energies dwell within every human. Besides water, it is also associated with the moon. Both the moon and water are related to feminine, or yin, energy.

It's no wonder that the location of the sacral chakra, for women, is the womb. This chakra corresponds to cycles and fluids within the body, which correlates to menstruation, yet another connection to femininity. The womb is the place of ultimate creation. This is where the link to creativity comes through in the sacral chakra. Like everything associated with the sacral chakra, this creativity is of a primal nature. It is creativity associated with giving birth and creating from deep within.

We can take the idea of creativity out of the body and use this same energy for birthing new ideas and creating from a primal space.

SACRAL CHAKRA CORRESPONDENCES

◁◠ TRADITIONAL HINDU CORRESPONDENCES ◡▷

- ◆ **Petals**: 6

- ◆ **Bija Mantra**: Vam

- ◆ **Color**: White

- ◆ **Element**: Water

◁◠ MODERN WESTERN CORRESPONDENCES ◡▷

- ◆ **Moon Phase**: First quarter, full moon

- ◆ **Element**: Water

- ◆ **Color**: Orange

- ◆ **Crystals**: Carnelian, opal, moonstone, garnet

- ◆ **Zodiac**: Scorpio, Cancer

- ◆ **Planets**: Moon, Pluto

- ◆ **Number**: 2

- ◆ **Plants**: Sandalwood, ylang-ylang, cinnamon

- ◆ **Runes**: Berkano, laguz

BALANCED SACRAL CHAKRA

A balanced sacral chakra is a satisfying gift. When your sacral chakra is open and balanced, you are able to enjoy and savor all of the gifts your physical body has to offer. You may be emotional, but you are able to work through your emotions in a way that allows you to be free and in flow with life.

Signs of a balanced sacral chakra:

♦ I delight in sensual and sexual play.

♦ I allow myself to experience my full range of emotions.

♦ I am highly creative.

♦ I love being around water.

♦ I enjoy fluid movement, especially dance.

OVERACTIVE SACRAL CHAKRA

An overactive sacral chakra may result in forming addictive patterns. Because this chakra deals with experiencing pleasure, it is quite common for it to become overactive. There are two sides to the overactive sacral chakra, the other being the ability to feel emotions too much. The current of emotions may be too much for highly sensitive people with an overactive sacral chakra.

Signs of an overactive sacral chakra:

♦ I am often controlled by my emotions.

♦ I have an addictive personality.

♦ Sometimes I'm manipulative.

♦ I feel everything, and it's overwhelming.

♦ I have unhealthy attachments to people.

TIPS FOR BALANCING AN OVERACTIVE SACRAL CHAKRA

♦ Wear or carry aquamarine. To help lift you out of addictive behaviors and soothe the sacral chakra.

♦ Work with the heart chakra for balancing your emotions.

♦ Try journaling and moving your body to work through difficult emotions.

UNDERACTIVE
SACRAL CHAKRA

In some societies, it's taboo and even frowned upon to discuss topics of sex. When you're brought up in a community like this, you will likely have blocks within the sacral chakra that you'll have to work through. It's common and to be expected to have a difficult time expressing your sensuality and emotions if you've grown up being told it's wrong or bad. Don't worry, there are gentle things you can do to begin to work with the energy of the sacral chakra that I'll share later in this chapter.

Signs of an underactive sacral chakra:

♦ I tend to be callous.

♦ I am detached from my emotions and the emotions of others.

♦ I find it difficult to express my desires.

♦ I harbor a deep belief that sexuality is wrong.

♦ I am unimaginative.

BALANCING AND OPENING YOUR SACRAL CHAKRA

Opening this chakra is filled with intense joy, but finding the balance within it is the tricky part. Emotions, pleasure, and sex can be difficult issues to talk about and work through. I assure you the benefits of doing so far outweigh neglecting this chakra.

When we suppress our desires and emotions, it can lead to a host of other problems. Lack of emotional expression may trigger an unhealthy or addictive relationship to sex. Also, suppressing your need for sensuality and sexual intimacy could lead to an inability to feel emotions.

Working with the element of water is one way to open the sacral chakra. I share a bath exercise later in this chapter, but any contact with water will help soothe and balance the sacral chakra. Here are other suggestions for working with water:

- ♦ Go swimming

- ♦ Take a bath or a shower

- ♦ Drink water

- ♦ Place the symbol for water (downward-pointed triangle) somewhere you'll see it regularly

- ♦ Visualize water flowing over you as you meditate

- ♦ Listen to ambient water sounds like waves crashing on a beach or rain

Movement is a vital force of water. When water is in its liquid state, it's always in motion. Dance is a powerful tool for activating the energy of the sacral chakra. Don't worry, you don't have to be a trained dancer to benefit from dance in this way. Simply turn on some music and allow your body to feel the rhythm of it and move. There's no right or wrong way to do this. Dancing in this way is intended to get you in touch with the primal energy of the sacral chakra.

·•◇ TIP ◁•·

The moon is associated with the element of water, femininity, and emotions. Working with lunar energy is a great way to open the sacral chakra. You can do this through journaling with the phases of the moon, dancing under the full moon, or attending a moon circle.

When the sacral chakra is open, you will feel your emotions more intensely. There will be some emotions that you're happy to feel more intensely and others that you'll probably be less excited about! To keep your sacral chakra balanced, you will need to find healthy ways to express intense emotions. For example, if you are feeling a lot of anger, you may need to exercise, paint, dance, or be expressive in another way to work the energy out of you. The point of this is not to dismiss unwanted feelings, but to feel them and process them out of the body. If you suppress your emotions, they will come out one way or another, but it may not be in a way you like.

HERBS FOR BALANCING YOUR SACRAL CHAKRA

Most warming herbs like cinnamon, ginger, and clove will serve you well for accessing the energy of the sacral chakra. Anything that builds heat inspires movement, which is why warming herbs are so helpful. These can be enjoyed as scents, eaten in food, or ingested in tea form. Scents associated with femininity like rose and ylang-ylang will help access your emotions. Lastly, sandalwood is a lovely warming scent that's associated with increased libido.

CRYSTALS TO BALANCE YOUR SACRAL CHAKRA

There are a handful of crystals you can work with to access the energy of the sacral chakra. Though many references suggest fiery and sunny stones for the sacral chakra, I believe it's important to honor the feminine and water aspects of this chakra. For this reason, I offer some of the more traditional fiery stones, but also stones that are associated with water, like moonstone and opal, for this chakra. Opal can be especially helpful for working with this chakra because physically it has a very high water content.

CRYSTALS FOR
THE SACRAL CHAKRA

CARNELIAN FOR VITALITY

Carnelian carries intense energy and is said to stimulate the sacral region. It can help increase sex drive, emotions, and creativity. Carry a piece of tumbled carnelian with you to help access the energy of the sacral chakra.

MOONSTONE FOR FEMININE ENERGY

Moonstone connects with the moon, the water element, and feminine energy. This is a gentler option compared to carnelian. Moonstone is helpful to work with when you're trying to get in touch with your emotions. Try meditating or taking a bath with moonstone nearby.

OPAL FOR CREATIVITY

Opal can be used in a few ways to access the sacral chakra. The rainbow of colors displayed by opal is said to inspire creativity. Opal also has a high water content and therefore corresponds to the water element. Opal is a more expensive option, but the energy of it is gentle enough that it can be worn as jewelry.

RED GARNET FOR PASSION

Red garnet is perfect for inspiring passion and sexual energy. It is often paired with the root chakra, and some of its qualities will undoubtedly serve the root chakra.

SCENTED BATH

If you don't have everything you need, don't let it stop you from enjoying this activity. Taking a bath on its own will help activate your sacral chakra. If you don't have a bath or don't like taking baths, don't worry, you can still enjoy this exercise as a scented shower. Most of the steps will work for a bath or a shower, but I offer some additional suggestions for performing this exercise as a shower after the steps below.

You'll need:

♦ A few drops of ylang-ylang and sandalwood essential oils. If you only have one of these, that's okay!

♦ Any size or shape of moonstone, carnelian, or garnet. Feel free to use one or all of these crystals.

♦ Candles, preferably orange or red in color

♦ Warming tea to drink like chai tea, ginger, or cinnamon

♦ Your favorite, feel-good, and soothing music

To experience:

1. Block off some time so you can experience your bath fully and tune into your body.

2. Draw your bath and add a few drops of each of the essential oils.

3. Place your crystal(s) next to the bath or directly in the bath (all of the suggested stones are safe to place in water).

4. Light your candles and place them near the bath.

5. Prepare your tea and turn on your music.

6. Sip your tea either before, during, or after your bath.

7. Try to connect fully with your body and the experience of enjoying a bath. You can do this by giving yourself a massage or using a salt or sugar scrub on your body.

8. Enjoy as long as you'd like!

If you are enjoying this as a shower, I suggest placing an essential oil diffuser with the oils of your choice near your shower along with the crystals and candles. All of the other steps can be practiced as outlined for the bath. If you are using any electrical devices like an essential oil diffuser or speakers, be sure to practice caution and ensure that all electrical devices are a safe distance from your bath or shower.

CHAPTER 4

THE SOLAR PLEXUS CHAKRA

MANIPURA

SPARKLING GEM

Your solar plexus chakra is a powerhouse of energy and transformation. It is located in the area above your belly button and below your sternum. Not surprisingly, the physical area of this chakra is a hotbed of activity within your body. Your digestive organs, which are continually transforming food into energy, all correlate to the solar plexus chakra. Your abdominal muscles, or core, also reside here and are a source of fire and energy necessary to perform physical activities.

Personal power, will, and intellect are all associated with this chakra. It is through the combination of energy transference and willpower that you're able to move up the chakra system.

The element associated with this chakra is fire. On an energetic level, manipura allows you to transform the dense energy of the two chakras below into intense, fiery energy. The Sanskrit translation of *manipura* varies from "lustrous gem" to "city of jewels." Either translation aptly describes the energy of this chakra. Manipura is glistening like a city of jewels, bright with energy.

ESSENCE

POWER, ENERGY, CONFIDENCE,
TRANSFORMATION, INTELLECT

MANTRAS

I CAN MANIFEST MY DESIRES.
INFINITE POWER LIES WITHIN ME.
I CAN TRANSFORM MY LIFE AT WILL.
I WILL ACCOMPLISH MY GOALS.
I AM CONFIDENT AND COURAGEOUS.

CONNECTING WITH THE SOLAR PLEXUS CHAKRA

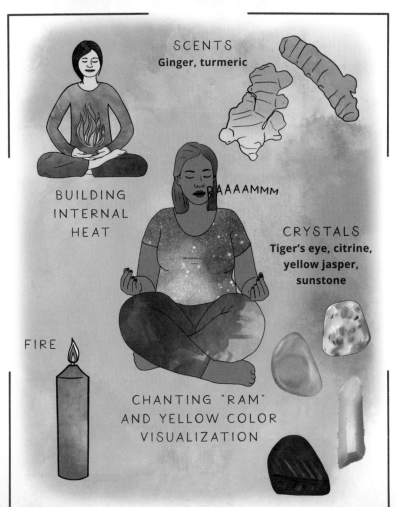

SCENTS
Ginger, turmeric

BUILDING INTERNAL HEAT

RAAAAMMM

CRYSTALS
Tiger's eye, citrine, yellow jasper, sunstone

FIRE

CHANTING "RAM" AND YELLOW COLOR VISUALIZATION

THE PURPOSE OF THE SOLAR PLEXUS CHAKRA

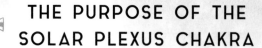

The purpose of the solar plexus chakra is to transform, energize, and empower you. Through the fires of the solar plexus, you're given everything you need to continue to raise your vibration and travel upward through the chakra system. Manipura provides you with energy to progress physically, mentally, and spiritually.

The solar plexus chakra provides transformative energy, enabling you to understand and bring meaning to your life. Through the root chakra, you found safety, and in the sacral chakra, you discovered your emotions. The solar plexus chakra brings fire to transform yourself and your reality. Within this chakra, you're given the tools to rise above your primal nature. Manipura grants you energy to learn, think, combine ideas, form beliefs, and share your thoughts with others.

THROUGH THE GLISTENING FIRE OF THE SOLAR PLEXUS CHAKRA, YOU HAVE ACCESS TO INFINITE POWER AND STRENGTH.

The solar plexus chakra is the seat of personal strength. Though many people think that willpower is something you're either born with or without, it is a practiced skill. Working with manipura will grant the focus and attention needed to see projects through to their end.

THE SOLAR PLEXUS CHAKRA AND FIRE

One of the primary goals of the physical practice of yoga, or asana, is to build internal heat. In Sanskrit, the term for fire is *agni*. If you've attended a yoga class, you may be able to relate to the inner fire it creates. The physical practice of yoga will often leave you feeling invigorated, full of energy, and maybe even transformed. In my opinion, this is one reason why the practice of yoga has become so popular: it lights a transformational fire within us that inspires and empowers.

Ancient yogis understood that the fires of transformation dwell within the core of the body, or the solar plexus region. When you ignite agni within the body, you light the fires of transformation. The physical practice of yoga is one tiny part of yoga philosophy. There are actually eight "limbs" of yoga. Ancient yogis knew that to sit through hours of meditation, one would need willpower, and a lot of it. The physical practice of yoga sparks the fire within. It gives its practitioners the necessary tools to progress through all eight limbs.

SOLAR PLEXUS CHAKRA CORRESPONDENCES

◄〜 TRADITIONAL HINDU CORRESPONDENCES 〜►

- ◆ **Petals**: 10
- ◆ **Bija Mantra**: Ram
- ◆ **Color**: Red
- ◆ **Element**: Fire

◄〜 MODERN WESTERN CORRESPONDENCES 〜►

- ◆ **Moon Phase**: Waxing gibbous
- ◆ **Element**: Fire
- ◆ **Color**: Yellow
- ◆ **Crystals**: Tiger's eye, yellow jasper, citrine, sunstone
- ◆ **Zodiac**: Aries, Leo
- ◆ **Planets**: Mars, Sun
- ◆ **Number**: 3
- ◆ **Plants**: Ginger, turmeric
- ◆ **Runes**: Sowilo, raidho

BALANCED SOLAR PLEXUS CHAKRA

When the solar plexus is balanced, and the energy is flowing, you experience a wellspring of motivation and focus. You have the personal power needed to accomplish tasks, both physical and mental. You have a sense of balance in your work because you have the intellectual wisdom to rest and recharge.

Signs of a balanced solar plexus chakra:

♦ I have unlimited energy available to me.

♦ I love learning new things.

♦ I consider myself intellectual.

♦ I am hardworking but know how to recharge and rest.

OVERACTIVE SOLAR PLEXUS CHAKRA

The overactive solar plexus chakra is quite common in our modern world. We see this expressed in power-hungry individuals, often leaders who strive to bend all things to their will. You can also see the overactive solar plexus chakra come through as overworking, a form of perceived control.

Signs of an overactive solar plexus chakra:

- ◆ I am hungry for power.

- ◆ I tend to be possessive and controlling.

- ◆ I push my beliefs on others.

- ◆ When I don't get what I want, I can be overly forceful.

- ◆ I am constantly overworking myself.

- ◆ I find it challenging to make time for rest.

TIPS FOR BALANCING AN OVERACTIVE SOLAR PLEXUS CHAKRA

- ◆ Wear or hold cooling stones that correspond to the water element, such as larimar and moonstone.

- ◆ Go for a swim or take a relaxing bath.

- ◆ Work with the heart chakra to find balance (see chapter 5).

UNDERACTIVE SOLAR PLEXUS CHAKRA

Someone with an underactive solar plexus chakra will likely feel the symptoms of it on a physical and energetic level. Though all of the chakras align with physical parts of the body, the solar plexus is uniquely linked to our physical energy. When the energy of manipura is deficient, our energy will be as well. Physically, deficiencies in the solar plexus are often present as digestive issues.

Signs of an underactive solar plexus chakra:

- ◆ I tire easily.

- ◆ My body feels weak.

- ◆ I have difficulty finishing projects.

- ◆ I have no desire to progress in my life.

- ◆ I have digestive problems often.

BALANCING AND OPENING YOUR SOLAR PLEXUS CHAKRA

Energy begets energy. Continuing a practice of building internal heat, through yoga or any other kind of physical activity, is a sure way to stoke the fires of manipura. There are pranayama (breathing) techniques that can also build internal heat in the same way. Just as air feeds fire, it will also feed your internal fire.

·•◊ TIP ◊•·

Working with candle magick is a great option to open the solar plexus chakra, because its corresponding element is fire. Yellow, orange, or red colored candles are ideal because they also correspond to the element of fire.

Because the solar plexus is also stimulated by intellectual work and the transformation of ideas, it can be beneficial to focus on acquiring knowledge and learning new things. When you learn new things that inspire and excite you, it sparks the fires of the solar plexus.

HERBS FOR BALANCING YOUR SOLAR PLEXUS CHAKRA

Because the solar plexus connects to the gut, working with healing herbs and food is an essential component of this chakra. As I shared earlier, the subtle body and the physical body are connected. If your solar plexus chakra is deficient, it could affect your gut health. If your gut health is poor, it could affect your solar plexus chakra. Ginger and turmeric are two great healing herbs that can help your digestive system.

If you feel like your solar plexus chakra is underactive or blocked, I encourage you to take a mental note of what you're eating and drinking throughout the day. You might even find it beneficial to keep a food journal, where you can record everything you consume and how you feel afterward. Keeping a food journal for this purpose is in no way related to dieting or calorie counting, but rather being mindful about how you feel after you eat. If you find that certain foods decrease your energy or upset your digestive system, consider removing them for a little while and notice how you feel.

CRYSTALS TO BALANCE YOUR SOLAR PLEXUS CHAKRA

Crystals for the solar plexus chakra vary from fiery to more subdued warming. Sometimes you need just a little boost to get you where you're going or to help you stay balanced as you finish a project. During other times, you might need a spark of intense energy to propel you out of old ways of thinking. Find crystals on the following page to aid your solar plexus chakra in all of these ways.

CRYSTALS FOR THE
SOLAR PLEXUS CHAKRA

YELLOW JASPER FOR BALANCED POWER

All forms of jasper carry grounding earth energy. Yellow jasper works well for seeing a project through to its end while remaining grounded and connected to the earth.

CITRINE FOR FIRE, ENERGY, AND TRANSFORMATION

Citrine offers a sweet and joyful energy boost. This crystal is both cleansing and warming. It will rejuvenate you by burning through old ways to inspire new ideas.

SUNSTONE TO INSPIRE INDEPENDENCE

Sunstone carries a vibration of fire, hence the name, and is especially helpful for increasing independence. Carry sunstone with you when you need the strength to embark on new journeys.

TIGER'S EYE FOR STRENGTH AND LOGIC

Tiger's eye is a well-rounded gem to work with. It offers power and protection and stimulates your logic. Tiger's eye can help you work through blocks within the solar plexus area.

GINGER AND TURMERIC GOLDEN MILK RECIPE

This recipe is an excellent way to warm and balance the solar plexus chakra and the gut. Ginger is wonderful for soothing an upset stomach. Turmeric comes with a variety of health benefits, including better digestion, and serves as an anti-inflammatory. Golden milk has become quite popular over the last few years, so if you don't want to make it, you can likely find a premade version in your local health food store.

You'll need:

♦ 1-inch (2.5 cm) piece fresh ginger

♦ 1-inch (2.5 cm) piece fresh turmeric

♦ 1 cup (240 ml) milk or milk alternative of choice

♦ 1 cinnamon stick (optional)

♦ 3 or 4 black peppercorns (optional)

♦ Honey or sweetener of choice to taste

To make:

1. Slice the ginger and turmeric into thin slices. You can leave the peel on or remove it.

2. Add the milk, ginger, turmeric, cinnamon stick (if using), and black peppercorns (if using) to a pan. Bring the milk to a low boil and simmer for about 10 minutes.

3. Strain the milk into a mug, discarding the solids.

4. Add your sweetener of choice to taste. Allow to cool slightly and enjoy!

CHAPTER 5

THE HEART CHAKRA

ANAHATA

UNSTRUCK

The heart chakra marks the point of perfect balance in the chakra system. The idea of balance is reflected in its name, the symbol itself, and the placement in the body. When we look at the heart chakra through a modern lens, this balance is expressed as love and coming together.

The Sanskrit translation of *anahata* is "unstruck." The literal translation of the heart chakra signifies the ability to experience two opposing forces and not be negatively affected, or "struck," by them. Instead, the dueling forces can join, enabling you to hold space for both of them. It is through the joining and coming together of opposing forces within the heart chakra that we reach the idea of love. When we are whole, we can give and receive love with ease.

The symbol for anahata is comprised of two overlapping triangles. The downward-pointing triangle represents feminine energy, and the upward-facing triangle represents masculine energy. The triangles join together to express a balance of energy. Anahata is the joining point of physical energy and spirit energy between the lower and the higher chakras.

THE HEART CHAKRA IS THE BALANCING POINT OF LOW VIBRATIONAL ENERGY FROM THE LOWER CHAKRAS AND HIGH VIBRATIONAL ENERGY FROM THE HIGHER CHAKRAS.

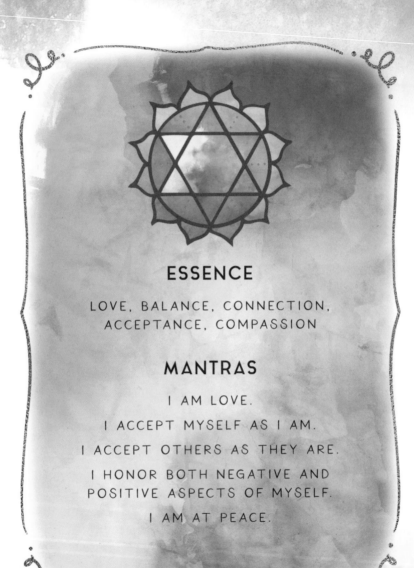

ESSENCE

LOVE, BALANCE, CONNECTION,
ACCEPTANCE, COMPASSION

MANTRAS

I AM LOVE.

I ACCEPT MYSELF AS I AM.

I ACCEPT OTHERS AS THEY ARE.

I HONOR BOTH NEGATIVE AND
POSITIVE ASPECTS OF MYSELF.

I AM AT PEACE.

CONNECTING WITH
THE HEART CHAKRA

CRYSTALS
Rose quartz, rhodonite, malachite, prehnite

PRACTICING
ACCEPTANCE

YAAAAMMM

SELF-CARE

SCENTS
Rose, bergamot

BREATHWORK

CHANTING "YAM"
AND GREEN OR
PINK COLOR
VISUALIZATION

BERGAMOT

THE PURPOSE OF
THE HEART CHAKRA

The heart chakra is your key to fully loving and accepting yourself and those around you, flaws and all. When your heart chakra is open and balanced, you'll have a deep inner knowing that opposing forces can live in the same space. The heart chakra enables you to forgive and love in the most trying circumstances.

The heart chakra takes self-love to the next level and gives you the tools needed to honor both your positive and your negative traits. The energy of the heart is not one of only seeing the world with "rose-colored glasses"; it's an energy of empathy and acceptance, too. It is within the heart chakra that we learn how to love unconditionally. When you have access to the energy of your heart chakra, you can live in a constant space of being "unstruck" and in perfect harmony with the dualities of the world. Can you imagine living in a world where people could love and accept others right where they are?

In regard to the other chakras, the heart chakra signifies a slight shift in energy. The heart chakra begins to lift us out of the physicality of the lower chakras and into the higher vibrations of the upper chakras.

THE HEART CHAKRA
AND BREATH

The element associated with the heart chakra is air. It is through the breath that we can access the energy of the heart chakra. Fortunately, breathing is something we all have a great deal of practice with already! The trick to working with the breath is learning how to manipulate and control it in a way that will energize the chakra system, namely the heart chakra. Most people keep their breath in the upper part of their chest, and holding the breath there sends signals to your brain that you're in distress. The simple act of becoming more aware of the breath can have a significant impact on your heart chakra.

The yogis and yoginis of the past and present are well aware of the power of breath. In Sanskrit, the word for breath is *prana*, which translates to "life force," and the practice of working with the breath is called pranayama, which means "control of the life force." If you've ever been to a yoga class, you may already have some experience with pranayama.

There are many pranayama techniques available. Practicing pranayama will not only enhance your connection to the heart chakra but will also improve your overall well-being. I share a simple pranayama technique on pages 92 to 93, but you can find even more with a quick Internet search.

HEART CHAKRA
CORRESPONDENCES

⊲◡ TRADITIONAL HINDU CORRESPONDENCES ◡▷

- ◆ **Petals**: 12
- ◆ **Bija Mantra**: Yam
- ◆ **Color**: Gray
- ◆ **Element**: Air

⊲◡ MODERN WESTERN CORRESPONDENCES ◡▷

- ◆ **Moon Phase**: Full moon
- ◆ **Element**: Air
- ◆ **Colors**: Green, pink
- ◆ **Crystals**: Rose quartz, rhodonite, prehnite, malachite
- ◆ **Zodiac**: Gemini, Libra
- ◆ **Planet**: Venus
- ◆ **Number**: 6
- ◆ **Plants**: Rose, hawthorn berry, bergamot
- ◆ **Runes**: Gebo, ingwaz

BALANCED HEART CHAKRA

When your heart chakra is balanced and open, you have a deep sense of love and acceptance for yourself. When you're able to love and accept your best qualities and your flaws, it radiates out to those around you.

Signs of a balanced heart chakra:

- ♦ I have a healthy self-care practice.

- ♦ I can set boundaries with love.

- ♦ I can see the good in anyone.

- ♦ I forgive myself and others with ease and grace.

- ♦ I feel a strong sense of balance in my life.

OVERACTIVE HEART CHAKRA

Those with an overactive heart chakra may identify with the terms "highly sensitive" or "empathic." Highly sensitive people can feel the energy of other people easily, which can make it hard to set firm boundaries. As someone who personally identifies as an empath, I'm not a stranger to having an overactive heart chakra.

Signs of an overactive heart chakra:

♦ I feel the emotions of others easily.

♦ I say "yes" when I want to say "no."

♦ I'm sensitive to the energy of others.

♦ I overextend myself to please others.

TIPS FOR BALANCING AN OVERACTIVE HEART CHAKRA

♦ Slowly work more self-care time into your schedule.

♦ Practice saying "no" to easy situations and work up to more difficult ones.

♦ Wear or carry protective crystals like hematite or black tourmaline to help protect your energy.

UNDERACTIVE HEART CHAKRA

It's just as common to find yourself in a position where your heart chakra is underactive. If you have an underactive heart chakra, you struggle with self-care and self-love. The lack of love for yourself easily overflows onto those around you, and you may find that you take offense quickly and hold on to resentments.

Signs of an underactive heart chakra:

♦ I have frequent negative self-talk.

♦ I hold on to things and have a difficult time forgiving.

♦ I feel like I don't deserve love.

♦ I compare myself to others often.

BALANCING AND OPENING YOUR HEART CHAKRA

Manipulation and control of your breath will give you access to the realm of the heart chakra. Beyond breath, implementing practices to seek balance in your life will also help. If you have an overactive heart chakra, learning how to set firm boundaries and protect your energy will help you focus more on yourself. If you have an underactive heart chakra, learning how to let go of resentments will help you find balance. If you find that you're stuck in either of these tendencies, your breath can help you break through them.

Becoming aware of your breathing is the best place to begin working with your breath. First, notice the length of your breath and where it is—in your chest or your lower belly. If you find that your breaths are often short and originating in the chest, try to elongate your breaths and send them deeper into your lower belly. The simple act of becoming more aware of the quality of your breath will make it easier for you to access your heart chakra. Try the more advanced, three-part breathing technique on pages 92 to 93.

CELEBRATE
WHAT BRINGS
YOU JOY.

HERBS FOR BALANCING YOUR HEART CHAKRA

Imbalances of the heart chakra often stem from an inability to love ourselves as we are. Most of us are brought up being exposed to media and advertisements that give false ideas about how we should act and look. The constant pressure to act and look perfect, all the time, can leave you with judgmental and negative self-talk. To send some love and acceptance back into the body, and to bring balance to the heart chakra, try the heart-healing body oil recipe on pages 94 to 95.

Here's a list of herbs that can be used for heart healing:

- ♦ Hawthorn berry
- ♦ Rose
- ♦ Hibiscus
- ♦ Bergamot
- ♦ Motherwort

CRYSTALS TO BALANCE YOUR HEART CHAKRA

Mother Earth has given us so many heart-healing and balancing crystals! Most green and pink stones will help the heart chakra in some way.

CRYSTALS FOR THE HEART CHAKRA

ROSE QUARTZ FOR LOVE

This crystal is the ultimate heart healer. Rose quartz will help balance all of your chakras but has a unique ability to remove blocks from the heart chakra. Try lying down and placing this gentle stone on your heart center.

RHODONITE FOR EMOTIONAL BALANCE

This crystal is ideal if you have an over- or underactive heart chakra. Rhodonite can help you stabilize your emotions and balance masculine and feminine energies. If you feel like your chakra is out of balance, carry or wear rhodonite for a couple of weeks.

MALACHITE FOR PROTECTION AND BLOCKS

This stone is both transformational and protective. If you have an overactive heart chakra, carry malachite with you for protection. If you have an underactive heart chakra, carry or place it on the heart to help work through blockages.

PREHNITE FOR HEALING

This crystal is exceptionally healing. Prehnite is ideal for anyone healing deep wounds and traumas. Receive the healing energy of prehnite by wearing it or keeping it on your nightstand while you sleep.

THREE-PART BREATH TO OPEN THE HEART CHAKRA

The three-part breath is a gentle pranayama technique that can be used to open the heart chakra and find balance. To perform this exercise, all you need is some quiet time to devote to focusing on your breath. Follow the steps below to get started.

1. Find a comfortable seated position. Become aware of your natural breathing. Simply notice it; don't judge it or try to change it.

2. When you're ready to begin, inhale slowly and send the air deep into your belly. Your eyes can be closed or remain open.

3. Next, begin filling your middle section with air. Imagine the air filling up your body as water fills a pitcher.

4. Lastly, feel the air filling all the way up to your chest.

5. Now, you will exhale your breath in the opposite order. Slowly begin releasing the breath from the chest.

6. Next, release the breath from the middle part of your body.

7. Lastly, feel the air leaving your lower belly.

8. Pause for a moment at the top and bottom of each breath.

9. Try to keep your inhales and exhales the same length. You can even count to ten (or any number that suits you) for each of your inhales and exhales.

10. Repeat this breath for 10 minutes or more.

11. When you're done, release all control over the breath and rest for a few moments to give yourself time to reflect and notice how you feel.

Optional enhancements:

♦ Hold a piece of rose quartz or any of the other stones mentioned in this chapter.

♦ Chant the Bija Mantra, "Yam," for the heart chakra on your exhale.

♦ Visualize green swirling energy around your heart chakra that grows with every inhale.

HEART-HEALING BODY OIL

Apply this oil to the body to nourish your skin and build in time for self-care. I suggest repeating a loving mantra, such as "I deserve love," "my body is perfect," or "I love and accept myself as I am," as you rub the oil on yourself. This oil is excellent to use after a bath or shower. A little goes a long way!

You'll need:

♦ A 8- to 12-ounce (240 to 360 ml) glass bottle

♦ 6 to 9 ounces (180 to 270 ml) of carrier oil like jojoba, sweet almond, or coconut oil

♦ 15 to 30 drops of bergamot essential oil

♦ 15 to 30 drops of ylang-ylang essential oil

♦ 15 to 30 drops of rose essential oil

♦ A few small pieces of rose quartz (optional)

To make:

1. Fill three-fourths of your glass bottle with your carrier oil.

2. Add the essential oils. You can use just one of the oils listed or any combination of them. Use more oil for a larger bottle and less for a smaller one.

3. If desired, place a few small pieces of rose quartz in your oil.

4. Hold the filled bottle of oil in your hands and visualize it being filled with loving energy.

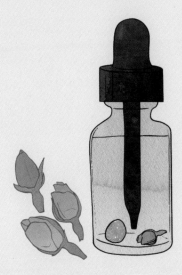

CHAPTER 6

THE THROAT CHAKRA

VISHUDDHA

PURIFICATION

The throat chakra marks an important point in the chakra system. It is the point at which we step away from the physical world into the realm of spirit. This chakra is considered a "gateway" to the upper chakras. The three lower chakras relate to earth energies, and the heart chakra is a place of balance between the upper and lower chakras. It is at the point of the fifth chakra that we move into the realm of vibrations and frequencies, specifically sound.

Vibrational frequencies and sound affect our physical and subtle bodies. Sound can raise your vibration, purify your energy, and heal your body. Purification is associated with this chakra because, to progress into the higher chakras, you must reach a state of truth and purity. The throat chakra is the key to purification and the higher chakras.

Ancient people and healers have known about the benefits of vibrational and sound healing since the beginning of time. Science is beginning to catch up to this. One example is a study performed in 2016 that linked Tibetan singing bowl meditation to a decrease in tension. I'm sure you've had similar experiences! Think of the last time you listened to one of your favorite songs. How did it shift your mood? Sound and vibrational healing are our first introduction to the realm of the unseen and spirit.

The physical placement of this chakra is in its name and is found in the throat. Physically, the throat chakra connects to the thyroid and throat area. Physical problems in these areas could point to an imbalance of the throat chakra.

ESSENCE

PURITY, TRUTH, HONESTY,
EXPRESSION, VOICE

MANTRAS

I EXPRESS MY TRUE SELF WITH EASE.

I AM SEEKING PURITY AND TRUTH.

I SPEAK HONESTLY.

I AM IN ALIGNMENT WITH MY
TRUE SELF.

MY UNIQUE VOICE MATTERS.

CONNECTING WITH THE THROAT CHAKRA

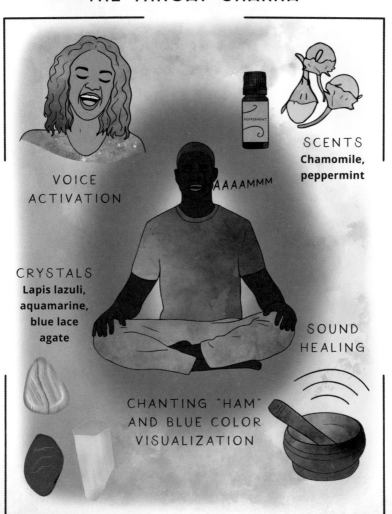

VOICE
ACTIVATION

AAAAMMM

SCENTS
Chamomile,
peppermint

CRYSTALS
Lapis lazuli,
aquamarine,
blue lace
agate

SOUND
HEALING

CHANTING "HAM"
AND BLUE COLOR
VISUALIZATION

THE PURPOSE OF
THE THROAT CHAKRA

The throat chakra gives you the tools you need to express yourself on a soul level, enabling you to communicate more authentically and listen more deeply. Visuddha lifts you out of the physical world and into the spirit world, which invites you to express yourself in the purest way possible. It would be difficult to progress to the higher chakras if you were not able to express yourself honestly.

At first glance, the throat chakra governs your ability to speak clearly and express yourself. When we explore the subtleties of visuddha, it takes on a deeper meaning. The Sanskrit translation of *visuddha* is "especially pure" or "to purify." As with every chakra before this chakra, the throat chakra wants to bring you one step closer to enlightenment, one step closer to the third eye chakra and the crown chakra. The throat chakra calls on you to connect to spirit, purify yourself, and express yourself authentically. This is highlighted by the original Hindu design of this chakra. The sixteen petals of the throat chakra contain the sixteen vowels of the Sanskrit language. In Sanskrit, the vowels represent spirit, and the consonants denote the physical world.

RAISE YOUR VIBRATION, AND THE
UNIVERSE WILL MEET YOU THERE.

This chakra may also serve as a tool to lift others up and into the higher chakras. Many spiritual teachers and speakers have highly developed throat chakras. When you are in alignment with your truth and develop your throat chakra, you will undoubtedly feel a strong pull to express these truths with others while simultaneously raising the vibration of our society as a whole.

THE THROAT CHAKRA AND SOUND

Entering the realm of the throat chakra will feel quite different than the chakras below it because you are now entering the realm of the spirit. As you'll see with all of the higher chakras, the throat included, accessing them will require a solid foundation in the lower chakras. When you feel like you're ready to access the energy of the throat chakra, the best way to do so is through sound.

All sound is vibration. Your vocal cords vibrate when you speak, the strings of a guitar vibrate to create music, and tuning forks must be struck to vibrate their sound outward. All sounds originate from different vibrational frequencies. When sound is used as a healing tool, it may be called sound healing, sound medicine, vibrational medicine, or frequency healing.

ENTRAINMENT

Vibrational healing is based on the idea of entrainment. When a vibrational wave comes close to a different vibrational wave, the waves will match each other, or entrain. Tuning forks, singing bowls, and other instruments can all be used in this way. When a healing vibratory sound wave hits your body, your body will try to entrain with that vibration.

A sound or vibration causes the air molecules around it to vibrate. This is how sound is carried from the source of vibration to your ear. Sound waves do not stop at your ear and have an effect on your entire body. For example, have you noticed that certain sounds make your whole body tighten up? Sounds like nails on a chalkboard or a metal utensil scraping a plate often have this effect. The quality of the sounds around you will have an impact on your mind, body, and spirit. This is why there are different seed sounds associated with the chakras. Each vibration has a distinct effect on the body and the subtle body.

There are countless ways to introduce sound into your practice to activate the throat chakra. I will share some techniques within this chapter, but you can also check out the list on page 108 for more ideas.

THROAT CHAKRA CORRESPONDENCES

◄〰 TRADITIONAL HINDU CORRESPONDENCES 〰►

♦ **Petals**: 16

♦ **Bija Mantra**: Ham

♦ **Color**: White

♦ **Element**: Ether (Spirit)

◄〰 MODERN WESTERN CORRESPONDENCES 〰►

♦ **Moon Phase**: Last quarter moon

♦ **Element**: Air

♦ **Colors**: Bright blue, turquoise

♦ **Crystals**: Lapis lazuli, aquamarine, blue lace agate

♦ **Zodiac**: Aquarius, Sagittarius

♦ **Planet**: Mercury

♦ **Number**: 5

♦ **Plants**: Peppermint, eucalyptus, chamomile

♦ **Rune**: Tiwaz

◦◁ BALANCED THROAT CHAKRA ▷◦·

When your throat chakra is balanced, your words are in perfect harmony with your true calling, and you're able to express yourself with ease. You have a sense of being in line with the Universe and sharing its truths. When you're able to communicate in this way, you're able to lift others up and raise their vibrations as well.

Signs of a balanced throat chakra:

- ◆ I speak truthfully and honestly.

- ◆ I work in a field that is in alignment with my beliefs.

- ◆ I am able to disagree with others in a loving way.

- ◆ I desire to listen to others.

- ◆ I express myself with ease and enjoy doing so.

- ◆ I feel energized when I share my gifts with others.

◦◁ OVERACTIVE THROAT CHAKRA ▷◦·

Up until this point in the chakra system, it is more common to experience overactive chakras. As I've mentioned, there are several shifts that begin to happen at the throat chakra, one of them being the tipping point of where it's more common to have an underactive higher chakra than an overactive one.

An overactive throat chakra will have you feeling like you're spinning with energy and want to share your beliefs with everyone, even when they may not want to hear it. Social butterflies and the like may find themselves in positions where their throat chakra needs tempering. If you resonate with any of the points below, you may have an overactive throat chakra.

Signs of an overactive throat chakra:

- ♦ I am extremely talkative.

- ♦ I push my beliefs on others.

- ♦ I am not a good listener.

- ♦ I may have an overactive thyroid.

TIPS FOR BALANCING AN OVERACTIVE THROAT CHAKRA

- ♦ Drink a cup of chamomile tea.

- ♦ Meditate with a piece of blue lace agate.

- ♦ Perform a grounding exercise, such as going for a walk in nature.

◦◁ UNDERACTIVE THROAT CHAKRA ▷◦

In a world that is primarily run by men, the underactive throat chakra is most often seen in women. From a young age, most women are sent messages that it's not okay to express their true feelings. Even though many women are breaking this cycle, the ability to speak honestly as a woman can still be incredibly difficult. Men can also have an underactive throat chakra, but I feel it's important to say that it is far more common in women so that we can continue to break the cycle of silence.

Signs of an underactive throat chakra:

- ◆ I have difficulty speaking honestly.

- ◆ I am unable to express my desires.

- ◆ I struggle with social anxiety.

- ◆ I have a fear of public speaking.

- ◆ I am not able to stand up for myself.

- ◆ I may have an underactive thyroid.

BALANCING AND OPENING YOUR THROAT CHAKRA

As mentioned, sound is the best medicine for accessing the energy of your throat chakra. In this section, I share specific ways that you can use the power of sound and vibrational healing to do this. Beyond sound, meditation is a great way to access the throat chakra and all of the upper chakras.

If you feel that your throat chakra is severely underactive, you might enjoy exposing yourself to a variety of sound healing techniques. Check out the list on the next page for suggestions. The techniques that don't involve making the sound with your voice are great starting points, because if you have a difficult time sharing your thoughts, you might feel awkward chanting or singing.

Working on the throat chakra by attending a sound-healing class is a gentle way to activate this chakra. Many yoga studios offer classes or experiences that involve sound healing. If attending a class is not feasible for you, there are countless free options that you can find online. One great free option is listening to frequencies designed to open the throat chakra.

You can use your voice to work with your throat chakra as well. Using your voice is a powerful healer for the throat chakra, and you may feel uncomfortable if yours has been very underactive. When you feel ready, I highly encourage you to try it!

Chanting is one of the easiest ways to activate your throat chakra. The seed sound for the throat chakra is "ham" and is perfect for chanting to open the throat chakra. The "a" of ham is pronounced like "au" of "aum." Singing or chanting a mantra aloud is another way to activate your throat chakra. If you feel that your throat chakra has been severely underactive, you might even find it helpful to yell.

SOUND-HEALING TECHNIQUES

- ◆ Singing bowls
- ◆ Tuning forks
- ◆ Binaural beats
- ◆ Frequency meditations
- ◆ Listening to or playing music
- ◆ Singing
- ◆ Chanting
- ◆ Yelling

HERBAL HEALING FOR BALANCING YOUR THROAT CHAKRA

Due to the location of the throat chakra, herbal teas are an excellent tool to help soothe and balance this chakra. Try any of the herbs listed below solo or in a blend for an herbal throat chakra tea.

♦ Peppermint

♦ Spearmint

♦ Marshmallow root

♦ Chamomile

♦ Slippery elm

CRYSTALS TO BALANCE YOUR THROAT CHAKRA

Most crystals that are blue in color will help you balance the throat chakra. I've shared a few on the next page to get you started, but there are many more! If you feel like your throat chakra needs a lot of balancing and opening and you want to explore other options, here are even more crystals to help: sodalite, kyanite, apatite, amazonite, turquoise, and azurite. Any of these crystals can be placed on the throat area while you lie down and relax to help soothe and open the throat chakra.

·◦◁ TIP ▷◦·

Due to the location of the throat chakra, wearing a crystal necklace with any of these crystals can be extremely beneficial for people who speak for a living or have a difficult time expressing themselves verbally.

CRYSTALS FOR THE THROAT CHAKRA

LAPIS LAZULI TO SPEAK YOUR TRUTH

Lapis lazuli is a potent throat chakra healer. This stone is ideal for people who use their throat chakra often, such as public speakers, singers, and teachers. Wear or carry some lapis lazuli the next time you need to have a difficult conversation.

AQUAMARINE TO PURIFY AND CONNECT WITH SPIRIT

Aquamarine is a high-vibrational stone that will cleanse and soothe the throat chakra. It helps you align with your higher self in a way that inspires authentic communication.

BLUE LACE AGATE TO GENTLY BALANCE THE THROAT CHAKRA

Blue lace agate is a gentle stone that can be used to balance the throat chakra. Carry some blue lace agate in your pocket for a week or hold it during meditation.

THROAT CHAKRA HERBAL TEA

You'll need:

- ◆ One to three of these herbs: peppermint, spearmint, marshmallow root, chamomile, and slippery elm

- ◆ A loose leaf tea strainer or empty tea bag

- ◆ Hot water

- ◆ Teacup or mug

- ◆ Something to cover your cup with, like a small plate

Follow these steps to create your throat chakra herbal tea:

1. Place approximately 1 tsp. of each of your herbs into your tea strainer. If you are using just one herb, you can use 2 tsp.

2. Place your tea infuser or tea bag into your cup.

3. Boil your water, about 1 cup (240ml), and carefully pour it into your cup after it begins to boil.

4. Allow your tea to steep for about 5 minutes. Place a small plate or tray over your cup as it steeps with the herbs inside. This helps keep all of the nutrients from the herbs in your tea.

5. Optional: place a smaller glass cup or vial into your tea with a throat chakra crystal of your choice (lapis, aquamarine, or blue lace agate are all great options). Let the glass with the crystal rest in the tea as it steeps. Be sure that the crystal does not actually touch your tea, it will still infuse your tea with its energy. Remove the glass holding the crystal before you enjoy your tea.

6. When your tea is cool enough to drink, hold it in both of your hands and ask that it soothe and balance your throat chakra. Drink and enjoy!

CHAPTER 7

THE THIRD EYE CHAKRA

AJNA

PERCEIVE

A jna is related to intuition and psychic ability. Its name in Sanskrit means "to perceive" or "to command." The third eye chakra will indeed help you with these things, but its power goes far beyond psychic vision. Your third eye chakra enables you to understand the world, rather than wondering and questioning. Information and ideas will seemingly manifest instantly in your mind's eye when you access the third eye chakra.

The importance of your third eye chakra is highlighted by the fact that it is where the ida and the pingala nadis meet (see page 21). Each nadi represents a different kind of energy, masculine and feminine, and they merge into one at the point of the third eye. The communion of energetic forces within the third eye chakra opens the door to psychic vision, the crown chakra, and enlightenment. The meeting of the ida and the pingala nadis may be one reason why there's a shift in the number of petals associated with this chakra, from sixteen in the throat chakra to only two.

The placement of the third eye chakra is in the center of the brow bone. It has a strong correlation to the pineal gland inside of the brain—so much so that some believe the pineal gland is the location of this chakra. Both of these options are acceptable placements. I'll discuss the importance of the pineal gland in greater detail later in this chapter, so you can decide for yourself.

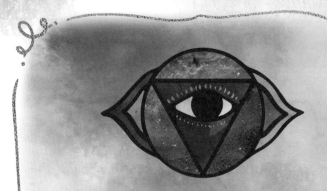

ESSENCE

PERCEPTION, INTUITION, KNOWING,
PEACE, VISION

MANTRAS

I AM CONNECTED TO MY
HIGHER SELF.

I TRUST DIVINE TIMING.

I CAN VISUALIZE MY HIGHEST
PURPOSE.

I AM PEACE.

THE ANSWERS I SEEK ARE WITHIN.

CONNECTING WITH THE THIRD EYE CHAKRA

CRYSTALS
Amethyst, fluorite, labradorite

SLEEP AND DARKNESS

MMMMM

SCENTS
Mugwort, cedar, clary sage, lavender

NATURAL LIGHT

CHANTING "OM" AND INDIGO COLOR VISUALIZATION

CLARY SAGE

THE PURPOSE OF THE
THIRD EYE CHAKRA

Your third eye chakra governs your mind and enhances your mental and psychic capacities. When you balance and open your third eye chakra, your understanding of the physical world and your inner world will both improve. The energy of your third eye chakra will enable you to focus more intently in all areas of your life. As your understanding and clarity of mind continue to expand, you may also find that the visions in your dreams intensify. You may even begin to receive psychic information as you sleep.

The clarity of mind, focus, and understanding of both your inner and your outer worlds that your third eye chakra provides are necessary for accessing the realm of the crown chakra. Ajna does more than offer a gateway to enlightenment. It also gives you the tools required to be able to handle the intense realm of the crown chakra. Any time you spend investing in balancing your third eye chakra will aid you in accessing your crown chakra.

THE THIRD EYE CHAKRA OPENS A
REALM OF CLARITY, INNER WISDOM,
AND INTUITION.

Accessing the energy of your third eye chakra will open your mind to new ways of "seeing" information. New avenues of energy frequencies will be available to you, granting you access to the psychic realm. How you experience psychic information may vary depending on your natural abilities. The third eye chakra primarily relates to clairvoyance (clear seeing), but you may experience psychic information through sounds (clairaudience) or sensations (clairsentience).

Beyond psychic information, all avenues of receiving knowledge and understanding will improve. As you work with the third eye chakra, you will find that answers come to you more quickly, you are more focused, and the actions of others even begin to make more sense.

CLAIRVOYANCE

Clairvoyance is the ability to see extrasensory information. Being clairvoyant is associated with seeing auras, the chakras, and visions of the future.

THE THIRD EYE CHAKRA
AND THE PINEAL GLAND

The third eye chakra corresponds to your pineal gland, which is tucked deep within your brain. The pineal gland actually functions much like a regular eye. In utero, the pineal gland begins to form just like an eye but eventually stops and remains as the pineal gland inside your brain. It's no coincidence that the third eye chakra is associated with this gland!

The pineal gland, as we currently understand it, is responsible for controlling melatonin and the body's circadian rhythm. It is a photosensitive gland, meaning it registers light. This is how the pineal gland knows when to release melatonin. The most interesting part about the connection between the third eye chakra and the pineal gland is that science doesn't yet fully understand the role of the pineal gland, although studies are beginning to indicate that increased melatonin is linked to decreased stress, increased dreams, and improved immune function.

The pineal gland can become calcified, which causes it to harden. The calcification of the pineal gland will not only affect your sleep but also limit the abilities of your third eye chakra. Overconsumption of fluoride is one of the primary causes of pineal gland calcification. Fluoride is commonly found in toothpaste, and even tap water. Fortunately, there are several techniques and foods to help you decalcify your pineal gland for optimal sleep and third eye function. I'll cover tips for healing the pineal gland later in this chapter.

THE PINEAL GLAND

♦ Is sensitive to light

♦ Releases melatonin

♦ Controls circadian rhythms

THIRD EYE CHAKRA CORRESPONDENCES

◄◡ TRADITIONAL HINDU CORRESPONDENCES ◡►

- ◆ **Petals**: 2
- ◆ **Bija Mantra**: Aum or OM
- ◆ **Color**: White
- ◆ **Element**: None

◄◡ MODERN WESTERN CORRESPONDENCES ◡►

- ◆ **Moon Phase**: Waning moon
- ◆ **Element**: Spirit
- ◆ **Colors**: Indigo, purple
- ◆ **Crystals**: Amethyst, fluorite, labradorite, snowflake obsidian
- ◆ **Zodiac**: Pisces, Aquarius
- ◆ **Planet**: Neptune
- ◆ **Number**: 11
- ◆ **Plants**: Mugwort, lavender, clary sage, cedarwood
- ◆ **Rune**: Kenaz

BALANCED THIRD EYE CHAKRA

If you have an open and balanced third eye chakra, you have a peaceful sense of clarity guiding you through every moment of your day. Being able to connect with any of the upper chakras is a gift! To maintain a balanced third eye chakra, you may find it helpful to implement grounding exercises into your practice regularly.

Signs of a balanced third eye chakra:

♦ I have a clear perception of the world around me.

♦ I trust my abilities and path.

♦ I am highly intuitive.

♦ I sometimes receive psychic visions.

OVERACTIVE THIRD EYE CHAKRA

If you were born with psychic gifts or are naturally intuitive, you might find yourself in a situation where your third eye chakra is overactive. It is certainly less common for any of the upper chakras to be overactive. Still, it is something that individuals with natural psychic gifts can experience.

Signs of an overactive third eye chakra:

♦ I have a constant flow of information in my mind.

♦ I feel overstimulated often.

♦ I get headaches regularly.

♦ I sometimes experience hallucinations.

♦ I am highly sensitive.

TIPS FOR BALANCING AN OVERACTIVE THIRD EYE CHAKRA

♦ Practice grounding exercises (see chapter 2).

♦ If you perform psychic work often, consider carrying or wearing grounding crystals.

♦ Get into your body. Do this by exercising, going for a walk, dancing, giving yourself a massage, or doing anything that involves moving your body.

UNDERACTIVE THIRD EYE CHAKRA

The health of your pineal gland is probably not something you think about often, so it is far more common to have an underactive third eye chakra. I believe that the third eye chakra is one of the more difficult chakras to access because there are so many outside factors that affect our pineal glands. If you are experiencing anything from the list below, be gentle with yourself on your road to healing your pineal gland and accessing the third eye chakra. It can take time, but it is worth every effort.

Signs of an underactive third eye chakra:

◆ I experience trouble sleeping or insomnia.

◆ I'm often confused or indecisive.

◆ I am not very imaginative.

◆ I have a poor memory.

◆ I have a lack of trust in myself.

BALANCING AND OPENING YOUR THIRD EYE CHAKRA

When you have a strong foundation in the lower chakras, you'll have the tools needed to access ajna. Meditation can help you access the clarity and psychic energy associated with the third eye. There are a variety of other tools that you can rely on as well. This will become even more important when you begin working with the crown chakra, but working with the third eye chakra will benefit from grounding work.

As I discussed previously, the pineal gland is uniquely linked to the third eye chakra. Focusing on the health and well-being of your pineal gland will help access its full potential. In our natural world, light pollution can cause real problems for the welfare of our pineal gland and circadian rhythms.

A free and simple way to help your pineal gland and your third eye chakra is total darkness. How often do you allow yourself to be in complete and total darkness? Even at night, many of us have light pollution that creeps in our windows. I'm sure you've also heard about the many adverse side-effects of looking at screens before bed. The light that comes from TVs and phones is blue, and blue light tells the pineal gland that it's time to be awake. All of these factors affect the well-being of your pineal gland and the third eye chakra.

To mitigate the use of screens and light pollution, give yourself time before bed to experience total darkness. Blackout shades or even a simple eye cover can help. If you really want to give your pineal gland a break, consider trying a sensory deprivation float tank. Your third eye and pineal gland will thank you!

Regular meditation is another free tool to help you access the third eye chakra. If you're new to meditation, I suggest trying to meditate for 1 to 2 minutes a day and then slowly work your way up. You can benefit from as little as 10 minutes a day of regular meditation. Countless free, guided meditations can be found online. All you really need to begin meditating is a few minutes a day to focus on your breath!

·◦◁ TIP ◁◦·

Thoughts will always be present during meditation. When thoughts come up, notice them, and then release them. You may find it helpful to imagine your thoughts floating by on a stream.

HEALING THE PINEAL GLAND

♦ Sleep in total darkness or allow time in total darkness by using a sensory deprivation float tank.

♦ Enjoy natural light for at least 5 minutes every day. Consider using a full spectrum light if you live somewhere with limited natural light.

♦ Consume chlorella and spirulina. Both of these can be found in a variety of forms including supplements and powders for drinks.

♦ Meditate regularly.

♦ No screen time at night.

♦ Limit fluoride intake.

♦ Gaze at a lit candle.

HERBS FOR BALANCING YOUR THIRD EYE CHAKRA

Lavender, clary sage, and mugwort are all known to help aid intuition and psychic abilities. Cedar and cedarwood are calming for the mind and may help soothe the pineal gland. These plants can be used in a variety of ways. Clary sage is commonly found as an essential oil, which can be diffused or diluted with a carrier oil and applied to the skin. Lavender and mugwort are easy to come by in dried form and can be burned loose or in a bundle for a fragrant smoke. Cedar can be found in oil form or dried.

Note: Mugwort should not be used by pregnant or nursing women.

CRYSTALS TO BALANCE YOUR THIRD EYE CHAKRA

Crystals are an excellent ally for working with the third eye. Any time you open yourself up to the spirit realm and psychic energy, it's essential to protect your energy. Of course, not all people have your best interests at heart, and there may be low-vibrational spirits that you encounter as well. Most of the crystals that I suggest in this section will not only help you open your third eye but will also offer protection. As your psychic abilities increase, and you become more exposed to other people's energy, so will your need to protect yourself.

AMETHYST FOR PEACE AND SLEEP

Amethyst is one of the queens of the crystal kingdom because she is both protective and calming. Amethyst can transmute fear and negativity into love. It will also help you sleep deeper.

LABRADORITE FOR INTUITION AND PROTECTION

Labradorite is a highly spiritual stone. Its multicolored flashes resonate with the third eye and will help you become more intuitive. Similar to amethyst, labradorite is also protective, especially for the aura.

FLUORITE FOR CLARITY

Fluorite is a crystal of clarity and can help clear and focus your mind. It can be a powerful aid for meditation and opening the third eye. Try holding some fluorite during your third eye meditation.

SNOWFLAKE OBSIDIAN FOR BALANCE AND GROUNDING

Snowflake obsidian is a perfect balance of protective grounding and uplifting energy. The white spots in it are a form of quartz, which will help keep all of your chakras balanced and open. Remaining grounded anytime you're working with an upper chakra will be beneficial.

BE OPEN TO THE
MESSAGES ALL
AROUND YOU.

THIRD EYE SMOKE WAND

This smoke wand is ideal to use for third eye meditations and practicing intuitive work.

You'll need:

- ◆ Lavender sprigs
- ◆ Mugwort sprigs
- ◆ Cedar sprigs
- ◆ Cotton string

To make:

1. Select your plants. You can use one, two, or all three from the list above. The amount that you use can vary as well. You can create a small smoke wand with a few pieces of each plant or a large one with more plant material.

2. You can partially dry your plants before wrapping them or dry them thoroughly after you've wrapped them. If you choose to dry them fully after you wrap them, it will take longer. If you dry the plants completely before wrapping them, they will be too crumbly.

3. Cut your plant pieces into a similar length or tapered, depending on your desired design. Arrange all of the pieces into a bundle. You may have to place them again as you wrap them, but this will give you an idea for how your end product will look.

4. With string, tie a knot at the bottom of your bundle. Wrap the string up and around your bundle so anything sticking out is held in place. Tie a knot at the top.

5. Let the herbs dry the rest of the way, about 2 weeks.

6. When your smoke wand is dry, light the end of it. Once it catches fire, blow it out, so it's just smoking. Waft the smoke around yourself and your space before practicing a third eye meditation.

CHAPTER 8

THE CROWN CHAKRA

SAHASRARA

THOUSAND-PETALED LOTUS

Your crown chakra combines all of the energy from the six previous chakras. It's your direct line to Cosmic Consciousness and the Divine. It's said to contain a spark of the Creator and be "the seat of the soul." When you access the energy of the crown chakra, you will feel at one with all that is and a deep connection to Source Energy. Source Energy can be replaced with any term that rings true for you, like: Goddess, God, Love, the Universe, etc.

This unique chakra, when completely open, is the final meeting point of Shiva and Shakti. Shakti is the Divine Feminine energy that is represented as kundalini energy within the root chakra. Shakti is related to the physical world and the earth. When Shakti awakes, she strives to work her way through each chakra until she reaches Shiva. Shiva is the Divine Masculine counterpart to Shakti, that represents the heavens. Their unique and opposing energy balance each other out. The crown chakra is their meeting point, and is the culmination of all the energy within the subtle body system. The Sanskrit translation for *sahasrara* is "thousand-petaled lotus," which aptly describes this intense convergence of energy. This expansive energy will lie dormant in many. The energy of Shiva will remain quietly sleeping in sahasrara, waiting for the energy of Shakti to awake him for their energetic union.

THE MERGING ENERGY THAT TAKES PLACE IN THE CROWN CHAKRA IS THE KEY TO TRANSCENDENCE, FREEDOM, AND ENLIGHTENMENT.

The position of the crown chakra differs slightly depending on the source. Ancient traditions place the crown chakra slightly above the head. In contrast, modern interpretations of the chakras place it at the very top of the head. Either placement is correct. On a physical level, the crown chakra connects to the pituitary gland, which may be why sahasrara is now associated with the top of the head.

SIGNS YOU'RE READY TO ACCESS YOUR CROWN CHAKRA

♦ I know how to ground myself and can do so with ease.

♦ My other chakras are healthy and balanced.

♦ I understand that we are all one.

♦ I meditate often and feel connected to the Universe.

ESSENCE

ONENESS, NOTHINGNESS, ALL,
DIVINE, ENLIGHTENMENT

MANTRAS

I AM ONE WITH THE UNIVERSE.

I AM NOTHING, AND I AM
EVERYTHING.

WE ARE ALL CONNECTED.

MY SOUL KNOWS NO BOUNDS.

I AM LIGHT.

CONNECTING WITH THE CROWN CHAKRA

CRYSTALS
Celestite, howlite, black tourmaline, clear quartz

NATURAL SPRING WATER

ENERGY WORK

SCENTS
Frankincense, myrrh

MEDITATION AND WHITE, VIOLET, OR RAINBOW LIGHT COLOR VISUALIZATION

THE PURPOSE OF
THE CROWN CHAKRA

The purpose of this chakra is to remind you of your divinity and help you detach from the ego. Feel free to substitute "Divine" with any term you prefer, like Goddess, God, the Universe, and so on. Sahasrara wants to remind you that the light of the Universe dwells within each of us. It is both internal and external. We are all connected.

Practically speaking, it's ideal to work with the crown chakra when you need to view things from a higher perspective. The energy of your crown chakra helps you detach from your worldly concerns and enables you to see struggles with a divine eye. Our biggest challenges are our best teachers, but when we're in the depths of pain or fear, it can be hard to see this. When you access the energy of your crown chakra, you're able to see all things, positive and negative, from the perspective of growth and balance.

·◦ TIP ◦·

Meditate on the crown chakra when you need to see something from a different perspective.

WHAT IS EGO?

Ego is a term used to describe your sense of self as it appears in the physical world. The ego is responsible for, among other things, labeling and judging. For example, statements such as "I am wealthy" or "I have black hair" come from the ego.

When you access the realm of the crown chakra, you transform into the conscious observer of your life. It is a subtle but profound shift. Most of the thoughts we have throughout the day are repeated from the day before. In our physical state, we are creatures of habit. When we can shift our perspective to that of the conscious observer, we gain distance from the ego.

Through the crown chakra, you witness your thoughts through the lens of Source Energy, and your actions follow suit. When you understand that you are cosmically connected to all things, you act in a way that honors all beings as pure love and light. This realization is how we will heal as a species and ultimately heal our planet.

THE CROWN CHAKRA
AND NOTHINGNESS

The crown chakra can be challenging to describe with words. Some refer to it as "the Void" because it is unexplainable and full of dualities. The realm of the crown chakra is everything and nothing simultaneously. As I mentioned above, sahasrara reminds us that the Divine is within us but also outside of us. As you can see from the correspondences, the crown chakra traditionally has no seed sound. The seed "sound" associated with it is actually silence, another reminder that the space of the crown chakra is one of nothingness.

In fact, early Hindu texts do not identify the crown chakra as a primary chakra. Instead, it was viewed as a point of energy culmination and connection to the Divine. It has since been assigned as one of the seven primary chakras.

CROWN CHAKRA CORRESPONDENCES

◁◡ TRADITIONAL HINDU CORRESPONDENCES ◡▷

- **Petals**: 1,000

- **Bija Mantra**: Silence

- **Color**: Glistening white

- **Element**: Nothing

◁◡ MODERN WESTERN CORRESPONDENCES ◡▷

- **Moon Phase**: New moon, full moon

- **Element**: Spirit

- **Colors**: Violet, gold, white, rainbow

- **Crystals**: Howlite, clear quartz, celestite

- **Zodiac**: Pisces, Aquarius

- **Planet**: Uranus

- **Number**: 1

- **Plants**: Frankincense, myrrh

- **Rune**: Ansuz

⊷⊲ BALANCED CROWN CHAKRAS ⊳⊶

A balanced and open crown chakra is a treasure to be cherished. Regular access to the energy of your crown chakra will require continual maintenance. With a balanced crown chakra, you can leave your body, resulting in moments of liberation from the physical world. Rather than being run by your ego, you'll experience moments of being an active observer of the ego. Although part of living as a physical being means having an ego, you'll have some separation from it.

Signs of a balanced crown chakra:

- ♦ I am a conscious observer of my ego.

- ♦ I can connect with higher states of consciousness.

- ♦ I see difficult situations from varying perspectives.

- ♦ I feel a sense of liberation and freedom, regardless of my current circumstances.

- ♦ I focus on meditation and prayer.

⊷⊲ OVERACTIVE CROWN CHAKRA ⊳⊶

Living in the realm of the crown chakra requires a profound letting go of worldly things. Activities like work, providing shelter for yourself, and eating would be at the bottom of your priority list. Though it's uncommon, it is possible to become absorbed by the blissful energy of the crown chakra. Some are born with a natural ability to access the higher chakras more easily. When you lack a solid foundation and do not have a strong sense of grounding, your crown chakra can become overactive.

Signs of an overactive crown chakra:

♦ I am detached from the physical world.

♦ I have no interest in eating.

♦ I do not like engaging with others.

♦ I have poor hygiene.

♦ I have no desire to generate income or work.

♦ I am extremely sensitive to the physical world.

TIPS FOR BALANCING AN OVERACTIVE CROWN CHAKRA

♦ Spend time outside.

♦ Eat regular meals high in protein.

♦ Wear or hold grounding crystals like hematite or red jasper.

♦ Focus on your root chakra.

UNDERACTIVE CROWN CHAKRA

It is far more common to find yourself with an underactive crown chakra. We live in a physical world, so it makes sense that we're naturally more connected to our lower chakras. Accessing the realm of the crown chakra requires much effort and directed action on our end.

Signs of an underactive crown chakra:

- ◆ I am often stuck in worry and fear.

- ◆ I'm unable to see the bigger picture in situations.

- ◆ I lack connection to the spirit realm, the Universe, God, Goddess, etc.

BALANCING AND OPENING YOUR CROWN CHAKRA

I suggest spending time working with all of your other chakras, especially your root chakra, before diving into these exercises. No harm will come to you, but you may find that trying to access the crown chakra without a strong foundation in the rest of your chakra system is frustrating. If you follow the principles of kundalini energy, the only way to access the higher states of consciousness in the crown chakra is through the kundalini energy rising from the root chakra. See the list on page 136 for suggestions that you might be ready to access the crown chakra.

Connecting with your crown chakra requires practice and patience. Frequent meditation and a strong foundation in the lower chakras are the keys to accessing the energy of your crown chakra. I suggest meditating every day for 10 minutes. Slowly work your way up to longer meditations over time. As your meditation journey deepens, you will likely experience small moments of pure bliss.

For most of us, the energy of the crown chakra is rarely available at all times. If you continue your meditation practice, you'll receive glimmers of freedom and enlightenment. The energy of the crown chakra is timeless and worth every effort, so even if you only have access to it for a moment, it can be life-changing. There are indeed enlightened beings who have mastered the realm of the crown chakra and have access to it at all times. Muhammad, Jesus, Buddha, Krishna, Lao Tzu, Rumi, and Paramahansa Yogananda are some examples of enlightened beings.

If you feel like the energy of the crown chakra is eluding you, that's normal. The crown chakra is often the last chakra experienced. Some may spend lifetimes trying to access the energy of the crown chakra.

·•◁ TIP ◁•·

If you're struggling to access your crown chakra, working with an energy healer is a great option. As you work through your other chakras, you may encounter blocks. You might be able to work through these blocks on your own, but the help of an energy worker can speed the process and be helpful. Energy healers can work on your subtle body in person or remotely.

◄◡ SPRING WATER FOR THE CROWN CHAKRA ◡►

Most foods are associated with the lower chakras, but that doesn't mean there's not something you can ingest to help you connect to your crown chakra. Water can be a powerful tool for changing your energy frequency. Natural spring water travels through streams in a way that causes it to become structured, much like a crystal, making it highly impressionable. That means you can bless it and store energy in it just like you would a crystal. Unlike a crystal, you can drink the water, and it will affect your entire body.

Search online to find a natural spring near you. If you don't have a natural spring nearby, an Internet search will yield several results for ways to create structured water.

Structured water can help your body and spirit in a variety of ways. If you're drinking it to connect with your crown chakra, you'll want to bless it with an energy that supports accessing the crown chakra. Drink your high-vibrational water anytime you'd like to connect with your crown chakra or before a crown chakra meditation.

HERBS FOR BALANCING YOUR CROWN CHAKRA

Frankincense and myrrh are both associated with accessing higher states of consciousness. For this reason, they can be powerful aids during crown chakra meditation.

CRYSTALS TO BALANCE YOUR CROWN CHAKRA

Although meditation is the most promising way to access the realm of the crown chakra, some crystals can be used in tandem with meditation to boost the effects. High-vibrational crystals like some of the ones I mention on the next page can also serve as great reminders of your connection to the cosmos.

CRYSTALS FOR THE CROWN CHAKRA

CLEAR QUARTZ FOR BALANCE

Clear quartz is known as the master healer and balancer. It is said to bring balance to all of the chakras. Hold clear quartz in each of your hands while you meditate on the crown chakra to help maintain the entire chakra system.

CELESTITE TO CONNECT TO THE SPIRIT REALM

Celestite is a high-vibrational stone that will help you vibrate at the same high frequency as the crown chakra. Hold some celestite in your hand as you meditate.

HOWLITE TO CALM YOUR MIND AND BODY

If you find that you're overworked or tense, working with howlite can help soothe your mind and body. Howlite is a slow-working stone and can be helpful to place on your nightstand or under your pillow.

GROUNDING CRYSTALS FOR AN OVERACTIVE CROWN CHAKRA

Place any grounding stone on your body or near you to help you stay rooted during crown chakra meditations. Grounding stones like onyx, hematite, black tourmaline, and red jasper are great options.

CROWN CHAKRA ACTIVATION OIL

This crown chakra activation oil smells amazing and serves as a reminder to your connection to your crown chakra. Rub the oil on your temples or take some sniffs from the bottle during meditation or throughout your day.

You'll need:

- Enough carrier oil (coconut, sweet almond, safflower, or jojoba oil) to fill two-thirds of your glass vial

- A glass jar or rollerball vial for oil

- 10 to 20 drops of frankincense or myrrh essential oil

- 1/4 teaspoon of dried lavender (optional)

- Small clear quartz crystals (optional)

To make:

1. Pour your carrier oil into your vial.

2. Add the essential oil, dried lavender (if using), and small quartz crystals (if using).

3. Hold the vial in your hands and imagine light from the cosmos enveloping it and blessing it with divine energy.

4. Before meditation, hold the vial up to your nose and take three deep breaths, then place a dab of oil on each of your temples.

CHAPTER 9

WORKING WITH CHAKRA ENERGY

Now that you have a firm understanding of the seven-chakra system, let's put it to use. When you tune in to the energy of your chakras, you may intuitively know when one is out of balance and needs attention. That said, we all experience extrasensory information differently. Some people intuitively know information about their chakras, while others are better at feeling energy. Some people even see the swirling energy of the chakra system in themselves and other people!

Experiencing extrasensory information is not something you either have or you don't. It is something that can be learned. The best starting point is to build on the foundation you already have. We all come into this world with psychic gifts, and it's a simple matter of determining what your natural gifts are. If you know that you already have a slight ability to feel energy, then begin working with chakras in that way. The different ways of feeling energy are called "clairs." The five most common clairs are listed on page 154. If you're unsure what kind of extrasensory ability you have, I suggest trying all of the exercises in this chapter.

Even if you know what kind of extrasensory perception you excel at, you may still enjoy trying the other exercises in this chapter. I consider myself clairsentient and can feel the energy of others very easily. I also love using my pendulum when performing energy and psychic work. There's no wrong way to go about this! I encourage you to experiment and play with a variety of techniques to experience the subtle body system and the chakras.

The techniques I offer in this chapter vary from sensing chakra energy to healing the chakras. Some of the exercises are better suited to working with your own energy; other exercises are better suited to working with the energy of other people. Working with energy is exciting, but it's also serious. We store so much energy in our physical and subtle bodies. If you are very sensitive to energy, it's possible that you will experience sensations or visualizations of stored trauma, memories, and even past life experiences within the subtle body. I share suggestions and protective measures in this chapter to aid you in your energy journey.

EXTRASENSORY PERCEPTIONS

- **Clairvoyance**: Clear seeing

- **Clairaudience**: Clear hearing

- **Clairsentience**: Clear feeling

- **Clairtangency**: Clear touching

- **Claircognizance**: Clear knowing

SENSING CHAKRA ENERGY WITH INTUITION

Your intuition can be used to both assess the health of the chakras and heal them. You will be able to tap into your intuitive abilities to visualize, feel, hear, or know the health of your chakras and use the power of your mind to open or balance your chakras. This technique appeals to all of the clairs, but will present itself in different ways, which I'll describe more below.

Follow the steps on pages 156 to 157 for a guided meditation to determine the health of your chakra system and enhance any chakras that appear to be deficient or overactive. The exercise on pages 156 to 157 is in depth and can be modified to focus on one chakra. It can even be used if you are out in public. For example, if you are preparing to do some public speaking, you can take a few quiet moments to visualize blue light around your throat chakra.

Your mind and your thoughts are incredibly powerful. Did you know that your brain is not very good at distinguishing between what you see with your eyes and what you visualize? When you imagine a ball in your mind, your brain thinks there is a real ball. This is something modern science has been able to show in recent years that healers have known for centuries. When you visualize the type of energy needed to balance a chakra, you can restore the chakra. Of course, this still takes time and practice. Similar to training physically, you will need to practice your ability to visualize as well. Although it may be possible for visualization to be a cure-all, it shouldn't replace recommendations from a qualified health practitioner.

INTUITIVE CHAKRA MEDITATION

Practice this meditation to determine the health of your chakras and to balance them.

1. Set aside 20 to 30 minutes of quiet time. Get comfortable either sitting or lying down.

2. Close your eyes and focus on your breathing for a couple of minutes.

3. Begin at your root chakra at the base of your spine.

4. Ask aloud or in your mind that the health of this chakra be revealed to you. Here are some suggestions for how information about your chakra could reveal itself to you based on your extrasensory abilities. My suggestions may vary, as everyone experiences extrasensory information differently, I suggest relying heavily on your intuition for determining the health of each chakra:

    ♦ **Clairvoyance**: You may see colors for each chakra in your mind's eye. The size and quality of the color indicates how active and healthy it is.

♦ **Clairaudience**: You may hear sounds for each chakra in your mind or aloud. The quality and volume of the sound will indicate how active and healthy it is.

♦ **Clairsentience**: You may sense a feeling for each chakra.

♦ **Clairtangency**: Clairtangents will benefit more from the next exercise (Feeling Chakra Energy), but similar to clairsentients, you may feel the health of your chakras in your body.

♦ **Claircognizance**: You will have an inner knowing about the health of each chakra.

5. As you focus on your root chakra, notice whether the information you're receiving about it increases, shrinks, or stays the same. If it shrinks, it indicates that the chakra is deficient. If it appears, sounds, or feels very large or loud, it may be overactive. If the sensations you're receiving about the root chakra sound, feel, or appear pleasant then the chakra is likely already balanced.

6. To balance the chakra, in your mind's eye, visualize it either shrinking or growing in size.

7. Repeat steps 3 to 6 for your remaining chakras. Visualize the corresponding chakra color for the chakra you are working with.

FEELING CHAKRA ENERGY

As I shared in the first chapter, the chakras are part of a much larger system, your subtle body. The energy of your chakras gives life to your aura, and your aura can reach several feet (2 to 3 m) out from your body. If you identify as clairtangent, clairsentient, an empath, or a highly sensitive person (HSP), you're likely already feeling this energy in yourself and other people. It's for this very reason that empaths and HSPs are so sensitive to being around large groups of people. They feel the energy of others that's radiating out from the subtle body. If you feel that you are clairsentient, or identify as an empath or HSP, this section is for you! I also cover some basic protection techniques to help you protect your subtle body.

There are smaller secondary chakras in your hands, which are highly sensitive to feeling energy and they're what we'll be using in this section to work with chakra energy. Before we dive into the exercise on pages 162 to 163, you'll need to determine which of your hands is your giving hand and which is your receiving hand. Your ida nadi represents the feminine or yin energy, and your pingala nadi represents masculine or yang energy. This same energy is represented in the chakras of your hands. Your receiving hand corresponds to feminine energy, and your giving hand corresponds to masculine energy. While working with the chakra system to determine the health of your chakras, you will want to work with your receiving hand because you are receiving information about the chakra. When you want to balance the energy of the chakras, you will want to work with your giving hand.

Your receiving hand is usually your nondominant hand (the left hand for most people). Your giving hand is usually your dominant hand (the right hand for most people).

> ·•ᴅ TIP ᴅ•·
>
> If you're having trouble feeling energy, try meditating for a little while. When you meditate, you raise your vibration. Subtle energy vibrates at a much higher frequency than solid matter, so boosting your vibration will help!

If you are ambidextrous and use both of your hands equally, you will need to do some experimenting. Try working with each hand to determine which of your hands is the giving hand and receiving hand. One way to do this is to place a quartz crystal in each hand and notice which hand feels a tingling or warming sensation. Or hold each hand a couple of inches (5 cm) away from your body and notice which hand feels a tingling or warming sensation.

If you're having trouble determining which hand is your giving hand and which is your receiving hand, that's okay! You can still perform the exercise in this section. Use any hand you'd like or both hands. Personally, I like to use both hands when feeling my energy or the energy of others. If I'm doing something more nuanced, like wanting to explore the health of a specific chakra, I switch to my receiving hand. Using both hands to feel energy can help navigate the subtle body system and locate the chakras.

Before you begin the exercise on pages 162 to 163, I suggest only performing energy work of this nature on yourself and not others, unless you have proper training. If you are highly sensitive to feeling energy, you are also highly susceptible to picking up the energy of others. If you are compelled to feel the energy of other people in this way, check out the suggestions on the next page for protecting your subtle body.

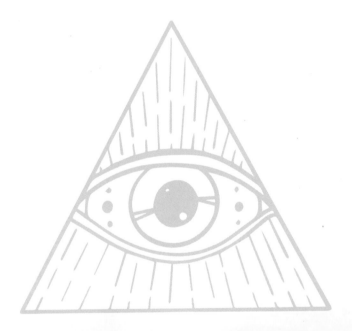

PROTECTION FOR THE SUBTLE BODY

These suggestions are ideal for anyone who identifies as empathic, highly sensitive, or clairsentient.

- ♦ Practice grounding exercises (see chapter 2).

- ♦ Carry or wear protective stones like black tourmaline, hematite, amethyst, and labradorite.

- ♦ Visualize a white shield of energy around your body for protection.

FEELING CHAKRA ENERGY EXERCISE

Practice this exercise to feel the energy of your chakras and assess their health. This activity works especially well for those who are clairtangent or clairsentient.

1. Set aside 20 to 30 minutes of quiet time. This exercise is best performed sitting down.

2. Close your eyes and focus on your breathing for a couple of minutes.

3. Rub your hands together for about 30 seconds. This will activate the chakras in your hands.

4. Stop rubbing your hands together and separate them slightly. You should feel a warm or tingling sensation in the centers of your palms.

5. Begin with a body scan. With your hands about 6 inches (15 cm) away from your body, start at the top of your head and slowly move your hands down the front of your body.

6. Notice whether there are any areas where you feel a slight tingle or push on your hands. It may also feel like a warming or tingling sensation that intensifies in certain regions. If you feel any of these sensations, it indicates an area of concentrated energy like a chakra.

7. As you perform the body scan, mentally take note of chakra areas that feel like they have less or more energy.

8. After you complete the body scan, you can go back to areas with your receiving hand to feel the quality of the energy.

PENDULUMS AND CHAKRA ENERGY

A pendulum is a weight at the end of a string. The weight on the end is usually pointed, but not always. Pendulums are available in a huge variety of sizes and styles, and you can even make your own! Pendulums have been used by mystics and healers for thousands of years and are one of the simplest tools for working with extrasensory information. This technique appeals to all five of the clairs, as you don't need to rely on your extrasensory abilities to use a pendulum. Think of your pendulum as an intermediary between you and your subconscious or the spirit world.

One way that the magick of pendulums is described is the ideomotor response. Essentially, your pendulum amplifies responses from your subconscious that would otherwise be undetectable. The subconscious is connected to your higher self, which is connected to the Universe (Goddess, God, Source Energy, or whatever you wish to call it).

From the perspective of working with the chakras, many people (myself included) believe that the pendulum itself can detect the subtle energy from the chakras. Your pendulum will move in the same way that the subtle energy of the chakra you're testing is moving. The spin of your chakras can help you determine the health and movement of each chakra.

Your pendulum will usually react in one of three ways when using it to read chakra energy. The pendulum will circle clockwise, counterclockwise, or be completely still. See the suggestions on page 166 for what each movement indicates about the chakras.

A pendulum is ideal for working with chakra energy on other people because it is literally hands off. I recommend working with a pendulum when you work with other people, especially people you don't know well, because you will not subject yourself to absorbing their energy.

The downside to working with a pendulum is that it is not ideal for working with your own energy, although there are still ways to do this. See page 167 for how to perform a pendulum chakra reading on someone else, and page 168 for suggestions on how to use a pendulum for working with your own chakras.

PENDULUM MOVEMENT MEANINGS

These are not firm guidelines but rather soft suggestions. Energy is unique and fluid. Use your intuition and trust your instincts when using this technique to determine chakra health.

- **Clockwise spin**: Chakra is healthy and open.

- **Very large clockwise spin**: Chakra may be overactive.

- **Counterclockwise spin**: Chakra may have a disruption or could be releasing negative energy.

- **No movement**: Chakra is blocked or has experienced extreme trauma.

PERFORMING CHAKRA READINGS WITH A PENDULUM

For this exercise, you'll need a pendulum, a pencil or pen, and paper.

1. Ensure that you have a comfortable space to perform the chakra reading. If the person you're reading is uncomfortable, it may be challenging to detect their energy.

2. Have the person lie down in a comfortable position.

3. Take a minute or two to calm yourself by closing your eyes and focusing on your breath.

4. Starting at the root chakra, place your pendulum about 3 inches (7.5 cm) above the person's body.

5. Wait for a few moments, allowing time for the pendulum to pick up the subtle energy of the chakra. The pendulum should begin to move within 10 to 20 seconds. If it hasn't moved in 30 seconds, the chakra is closed or blocked.

6. Record your findings for each chakra after receiving an answer.

7. When you've completed each chakra, you can share your findings with the participant.

PERFORMING CHAKRA READINGS ON YOURSELF

To perform a chakra reading similar to the one on page 167 on yourself, you will need to use a slightly different technique. It's nearly impossible to hold a pendulum over each of your chakras and be able to see the direction in which it's circling. So, to read your chakras, follow the steps below. You will need a drawing of a person or a list of chakras. You can use the graphic on the next page to perform a personal chakra reading using a pendulum.

1. Hold the pendulum over a drawing of a person, or a list of chakras.

2. Follow the same steps suggested for performing a chakra reading on someone else (on page 167), but the difference is you'll be holding the pendulum over your drawing.

3. As you perform this, ask your pendulum, "is my root chakra open?" and repeat the question with each chakra.

When you use the pendulum technique on someone else, the pendulum senses the subtle energy, which causes it to circle. When you perform a pendulum reading on yourself, you rely on the ideomotor response for your answers. Both are valid techniques.

CHAKRA PENDULUM DIAGRAM

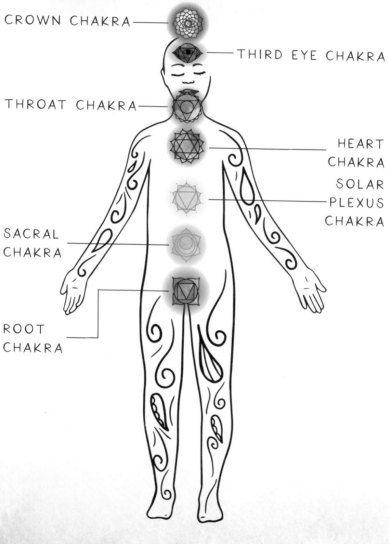

CROWN CHAKRA

THIRD EYE CHAKRA

THROAT CHAKRA

HEART CHAKRA

SOLAR PLEXUS CHAKRA

SACRAL CHAKRA

ROOT CHAKRA

I hope you're feeling empowered to access, assess, and heal the energy of your chakras! As you become more comfortable using these techniques, you may find that you rely on them quite often. Your ability to visualize is always available to you, and pendulums are very mobile! Don't be afraid to access and utilize the energy of your subtle body system to enrich your life and the lives of others.

MESSAGE FROM THE AUTHOR

There are layers of energy within you, each with a divinely inspired purpose, to bring you back into alignment with the cosmos.

The chakra system is your internal compass, calling you inward. Each chakra is a guide, reminding you of who you are, why you are here, and where you came from. Each chakra entices you with moments of bliss and enlightenment to propel you closer to your truth.

Never give up. Continue to dance with the energy within you, even when it's challenging. Every step brings you closer to merging with the light of the Universe. Everything you need is already within you.

Love 🖤 Light

Cassie

THANK YOU

Endless gratitude to those who made this book series possible! Thank you to all of the sweet souls at Quarto Publishing, especially to my editor, Keyla. Thank you to my designer, Sydney, who's been a creative force for Zenned Out since its inception many years ago. Sincere gratitude to my infinitely patient husband who, unwaveringly and lovingly, supports every new journey I embark on. Eternal gratitude to my guides on the other side, including my sweet grandmother and father. Special thanks to the following amazing humans for being my chakra models, Jen Isabel Friend (sacral chakra), Mallory Wingo (heart chakra), and Evangeline Summerville (third eye chakra).

Thank you to every single one of my fans, followers, and supporters. I see you, and I love you. You light me up every day and give me the energy to continue sharing my gifts.

Love 💜 Light

Cassie

ABOUT THE AUTHOR

Cassie Uhl is an artist, author, empath, and the lead Goddess of her business Zenned Out. She created Zenned Out with the mission to build a brand that normalizes spirituality. It is her goal to offer accessible information to enable you to understand a variety of spiritual practices and put them into action. She provides an abundance of free information and printable tools on her blog at ZennedOut.com/Blog.

Cassie has been meditating and working with her energy since her teenage years. In 2012, she expanded her spiritual practice by receiving her 200 Hour Yoga Teacher Training License. She continues to explore and grow her spiritual knowledge and share ways for you to dive deeper into yours.

Through Zenned Out, Cassie has self-published her best-selling *Goddess Discovery Books* and oracle card deck, *The Ritual Deck*. Her work and writing have been featured at Astrology.com, *Goddess Provisions*, *Women's Day Magazine*, and *The Cosmic Calling Podcast*. Learn more about Cassie and her other products at ZennedOut.com.

·•◊ REFERENCES ◊•·

Avalon, Arthur. *The Serpent Power: The Secrets of Tantric and Shakti Yoga*. New York: Dover Publications, 1974.

Dale, Cyndi. *Llewellyn's Complete Book of Chakras: Your Definitive Source of Energy Center Knowledge for Health, Happiness, and Spiritual Evolution*. Woodbury, MN: Llewellyn Publications, 2018.

Dale, Cyndi. *The Subtle Body: An Encyclopedia of Your Energetic Anatomy*. Boulder, CO: Sounds True, 2009.

Goswami, Shyam Sundar. *Layayoga: The Definitive Guide to the Chakras and Kundalini*. Rochester, VT: Inner Traditions,1999.

Hall, Judy. *The Crystal Bible: A Definitive Guide to Crystals*. Blue Ash, OH: Walking Stick Press, 2003.

Judith, Anodea. *Wheels of Life: The Classic Guide to the Chakra System*. Woodbury, MN: Llewellyn Publications, 1987.

Kynes, Sandra. *Llewellyn's Complete Book of Correspondences: A Comprehensive & Cross-Referenced Resource for Pagans & Wiccans*. Woodbury, MN: Llewellyn Publications, 2013.

Leadbeater, C. W. *The Chakras*. Wheaton, IL: Theosophical Publishing House, 2013.

Mercier, Patricia. *The Chakra Bible: The Definitive Guide to Working with Chakras*. New York: Sterling Publishing, 2007.

Satchidananda, Sri Swami. *The Yoga Sutras of Patanjali*. Buckingham, VA: Integral Yoga Publications, 1978.

Uhl, Cassie. *The Goddess Discovery Book: Awaken Your Inner Power*. Tempe, AZ: Zenned Out, 2017.

Webster, Richard. *Pendulum Magic for Beginners: Power to Achieve All Goals*. Woodbury, MN: Llewellyn Publications, 2002.